on tra

Blue Öyster Cult

every album, every song

Jacob Holm-Lupo

Sonicbond Publishing Limited
www.sonicbondpublishing.co.uk
Email: info@sonicbondpublishing.co.uk

First Published in the United Kingdom 2019
First Published in the United States 2019

British Library Cataloguing in Publication Data:
A Catalogue record for this book is available from the British Library

Copyright Jacob Holm-Lupo 2019

ISBN 978-1-78952-007-1

The rights of Jacob Holm-Lupo to be identified as the authors of this work have been asserted by them in accordance with the Copyright, Designs and patents Act 1988. All rights reserved. No part of this publication may be reproduced, stored in a retrieval system or transmitted in any form or by any means, electronic, mechanical, photocopying, recording or otherwise, without prior permission in writing from Sonicbond Publishing Limited

Typset in ITC Garamond & Berthold Akzidenz Grotesk
Printed and bound in England

Graphic design and typesetting: Full Moon Media

Second edition, July 2019

My gratitude to Teresa, Gabriel and Ina
for their patience while I was geeking out making this book.

Dedicated to my fellow agent of fortune, Bjarne.

on track ...
Blue Öyster Cult

Contents

Introduction 6
1 A Brief History 8
2 A plot of knives: Blue Öyster Cult 10
3 Echoes of empires: Tyranny and Mutation 18
4 Forest keys and whirlwind cold: Secret Treaties 28
5 Don't report this: Agents of Fortune 41
6 The station of night: Spectres 54
7 If you wanna face the music: Mirrors 65
8 New worlds waiting in the skies: Cultösaurus Erectus 75
9 Home in the darkness: Fire of Unknown Origin 84
10 At the clover-leaf junction: Revölution by Night 97
11 Do you know Jacques Cousteau?: Club Ninja 108
12 Dance a Don Pedro: Imaginos 120
13 A change in the weather: Heaven Forbid 139
14 Are you in the pocket of the moment?: Curse of the Hidden Mirror ... 148
Appendix: The Live Recordings 155
Bibliography 158

Introduction

For me it all started when I was thirteen. I'd been looking at this one album down at the local record store for a few weeks. The band's name, the album title and the cover drew me in, but it took me a while to work up the nerve to buy it. The band's name was Blue Öyster Cult, the album was titled *Secret Treaties* and the cover was a black and white drawing of a Messerschmitt jet fighter surrounded by some dubious fellows.

In the end I did work up the nerve to buy it, even though in that period of my life I was more in the habit of buying prog rock albums. Typical '80s middle class geek. I came home from the store, pulled out the inner sleeve, with a slightly altered colour version of the cover. And a text. This is what the text said:

> Rossignol's curious, albeit simply titled book, 'The Origins of a World War', spoke in terms of 'Secret Treaties', drawn up between the Ambassadors from Plutonia and Desdinova the foreign minister. These treaties founded a secret science from the stars. Astronomy. The career of evil.

I was sold. I put the platter on. And I was twice sold.

Blue Öyster Cult is a band that many people have heard, perhaps without knowing the band's name. Their hits, particularly '(Don't Fear) The Reaper' and 'Burnin' For You', are classic rock radio staples. And even though they are not A-listers, like Deep Purple or Black Sabbath, their name conjures awe and respect among hard rock aficionados, and the longevity of their career is itself a testament to the quality of their output. More significantly, and peculiarly, they are one of very few hard rock bands to enjoy the admiration of serious rock critics. In a genre that usually inspires the most creative heights of scorn and ridicule among rock critics, Blue Öyster Cult have managed to earn the respect and admiration of the rock press and discerning music fans, something that happened from day one. 'The thinking man's heavy metal' is a moniker that has followed the band since the '70s and occurs in countless reviews of the band.

There are two main reasons for this. One is that the band had an extremely diverse musical background, from folk rock via blues and psychedelia to Latin jazz. This meant that once the band settled on their chosen genre, a highly mutated form of hard rock, they brought all these elements with them and created something so eclectic and colourful that it completely transcended the genre. Especially from 1972 to 1977 there was a jazzy swing to their music that does not exist in any other hard rock band, and the boys also enjoyed the occasional arcane chord change (they have been known to rip the odd trick from the Steely Dan chord book) and progressive rock runs worthy of King Crimson. So that's one part of the puzzle. They simply had a much wider musical register to play on than their peers.

The other key to Blue Öyster Cult's, shall we say, dignified status, is the lyrics. As we shall see later in this book, the concept of the band was dreamed up by rock philosopher/esoteric poet/record producer Sandy Pearlman. And the lyrical presentation of the band was extremely important to this concept. From the very first album to the very last, lyrics have been a focal point for the band. Literary figures like Pearlman himself, Richard Meltzer, Patti Smith, Eric von Lustbader, Jim Carroll, John Shirley and many others have contributed to the band's lyrical canon. There are many interesting literary strains to be traced within the band's songs, from Pearlman's Lovecraftian Imaginos mythos to Patti Smith's occult punk poetry and Richard Meltzer's surrealist wordplay. Naturally, this is worlds, if not universes removed from your usual hard rock lyrics, with its tropes of evil gypsy women and hard-livin' men. All this made Blue Öyster Cult a band apart, a group of hard rock intellectuals removed from the bread & butter common ground of the genre. And this made them critics' darlings, even through their 'difficult years'.

One final element needs to be mentioned to explain the Cult's rarefied status. That is the glint in the eye, the tongue in cheek, that the Öyster boys have always had. Because the mixture of heady, sophisticated music, literary references and a heavy metal image does not always assure you a warm welcome in the hallowed halls of the rock snobs. One need only look to Rush for confirmation. But this one last twist, the sense that Blue Öyster Cult never took themselves 100% seriously, that they had a sort of post-modern self-consciousness about the fact that what they were doing was slightly ridiculous, helped endear them to people far outside the hard rock mainstream.

In this book I will endeavour to give an overview of the band's fascinating output, with commentaries both from myself and people in and around the band. We'll do it album by album, song by song. I will attempt to be fair – some will think I am too fair – but I will also offer opinion. My basic conviction is that every BÖC album offers something interesting. There are peaks and dips in their career, but they have never put out a dull album. I will not be giving exactly equal time to each album, because there is simply more to tell about some albums, like *Imaginos*, while others have less stories surrounding them.

Interspersed with facts and observations will be commentaries both from band members and people surrounding the band. Some will be sourced from past interviews, and these will be written in the past tense (Eric said), while my own interviews will be in the present tense.

I have been particularly fortunate to get valuable commentary from the world's foremost BÖC expert, Bolle Gregmar, high protector of the Museum of Cult, and from the band's most recent lyricist, John Shirley. My warmest thanks to them.

Sandy Pearlman unfortunately passed away in 2016. But in 2003-4 I was in touch with him for a period in connection with one of my own projects, and we had some long phone conversations where *Imaginos*, among other things, was discussed. Some of my information in the *Imaginos* chapter is drawn from these conversations.

Last but not least I must mention Martin Popoff's very extensive Blue Öyster Cult book *Agents of Fortune*. I am indebted to some of his forensic work there.

Now, let us turn to the subject at hand. Ladies and gentlemen, from New York City, the amazing Blue Öyster Cult!

7

Chapter 1: A brief history

The early history of Blue Öyster Cult is long and complicated, and I will not get into the nitty gritty of personnel changes or relocations to new band houses. We'll keep this neat, and deal with the broad strokes that help us understand where the band was coming from.

The group originated on Long Island, where most of the members found themselves at one point or another in the late '60s. Guitarist Donald 'Buck Dharma' Roeser grew up there, son of a saxophone playing father. By his own admission he had no real ambition to be a big-time musician, but played bars and dives, at one point even backing Chuck Berry. Like all the Blue Öyster Cult boys he was a college kid, attending New York's Clarkson University. It was during his college time that he met the Bouchard brothers, eventually ending up playing with Albert Bouchard in a few bands leaning towards the jammy end of the blues.

Albert and Joe Bouchard grew up in Clayton, New York, both deeply interested in music from an early age. Both took piano lessons in their youth, and Joe would go on to formalise this with classical studies. Albert played drums in a number of bands, and had Gene Krupa as his idol, which explains his particular swing which will be mentioned often in this book. Joe was the one with the music theory and the thoughtful approach, and he spent some of his time playing keyboards in surf bands before switching to bass. Joe and Albert were both well-versed in '60s pop, listening to The Shadows, The Beach Boys, The Ventures and The Beatles.

Albert and Donald both dropped out of college eventually but kept playing together, and in the end they formed the Soft White Underbelly, a band that would see a lot of members come and go. Allen Lanier, a well-read, Euro-phile Manhattan kid who was attending the University of North Carolina, drifted into the fold. And Albert's brother Joe, fresh off a stint with a Latin jazz band, replaced Soft White Underbelly's original bass player, Andy Winters.

Eric Bloom, who grew up in Queens and was a man about town with lots of plans and schemes, was at this time playing in a band called Lost And Found, with his future songwriting collaborator John Trivers. He also worked at a local Sam Ash music store, and it was here, in 1968, that he was recruited by Soft White Underbelly to be their PA guy. Several members of the band walked into the store and noticed a cool picture of Eric's band on the wall. They recognized the band and struck up a conversation with Eric that ended with him landing the gig with the band. But not, mind you, as the singer. That would come a bit later.

Sandy Pearlman also hailed from Queens and graduated from Long Island's Stony Brook University in 1966. A young intellectual and a bit of a visionary, Sandy saw the burgeoning rock explosion from a metaphysical point of view and was interested in the philosophical and political ramifications of rock music. Armed with ambition, a head full of esoteric writing (he read anything from Jewish mysticism to H. P. Lovecraft to post-modernist theory) and a knack for deal-making, he took it upon himself to manage Soft White Underbelly. Although 'manage' is too weak a term. He moulded, invented, and reinvented the band.

Soft White Underbelly eventually got a contract with Elektra and recorded two entire albums that never got released. Mixing psychedelic rock, folk rock and a bit of progressive adventurousness, the albums were musically interesting, but Elektra did not like the singer, Les Braunstein, and was ready to drop the band. The band had its own problems with Les, and let their PA guy, Eric try the mic. That did the trick.

After some name changes (first Stalk-Forrest Group, then Oaxaca) and re-thinkings, Columbia's product manager Murray Krugman was approached by Sandy Pearlman. Together they decided that the way forward for the band was a drastic change in image and music. Black Sabbath was a current buzzword in the biz, and Sandy and Murray thought their boys could pull off becoming America's Black Sabbath.

With a new strategy, a new image and stronger material in the bag, Murray Krugman convinced Columbia to give the band a special audition. This legendary audition was attended by label boss Clive Davis as well as A-list musicians like Harry Nilsson and Blood, Sweat and Tears drummer Bobby Columby. The band were nervous, and by their own admission performed a hectic set at too high tempos, but Clive Davis liked what he heard, especially an early version of 'Then Came the Last Days of May' – and the rest is history.

In the lead-up to the recording of the first album, Sandy and the boys polished their new philosophy and image. The hippies and the jam bands are out, said Sandy. You guys are the anti-hippies, the dark side of rock'n'roll. Sandy brought in fellow visionaries like poet and wild man Richard Meltzer to help out with lyrics. Sandy himself also wrote lyrics. His texts were tied to a cosmic poem he was working on called *The Soft Doctrines of Immaginos*. It was heady stuff, and coupled with the band's new music, featuring heavy riffs reminiscent of Black Sabbath and King Crimson, the band slowly found the magic formula that would define their first three albums.

Chapter 2: A Plot of Knives
Blue Öyster Cult (Columbia, 1972)
Personnel:
Eric Bloom: vocals, stun guitar, keyboards
Albert Bouchard: drums, vocals
Joe Bouchard: bass, vocals
Allen Lanier: rhythm guitar, keyboards
Donald "Buck Dharma" Roeser: lead guitar, vocals
Produced at The Warehouse, New York, October 1971 by Sandy Pearlman, Murray Krugman and David Lucas
Release date: January 1972
Highest chart places: 172 (US)
Running time: 36:48

Blue Öyster Cult's debut album seems in some ways to have come out of nowhere, an intimidating, intense explosion of urban angst, futuristic nightmares and occult biker-lore. It would not be untrue to say that nothing like it had ever been heard before. On the other hand, it really did not come out of a vacuum, and the band's influences are in fact audible all over the record. There are countless Doorsian moments, from Lanier's bubbling organ via the Bouchard brothers' jazzy swing and Donald 'Buck Dharma' Roeser's occasionally laidback and Krieger-like guitar - and not least Eric Bloom's theatrical and dramatic vocal delivery, sounding at times like Jim Morrison possessed by mischievous demons. There are also the obvious nods to Black Sabbath, who Pearlman was so keen for Blue Öyster Cult to emulate. And let's not forget that unmistakable East Coast vibe that smacks of The Velvet Underground. Digging deeper you can even hear strains of the opposite coast, psych-influences like The Grateful Dead and Quicksilver Messenger Service.

In short, the band's eponymous debut album was both a culmination of everything the musicians had absorbed and learned up to that point, and a bold, new vision of something entirely their own.

'Transmaniacon MC' (Eric Bloom, Albert Bouchard, Donald "Buck Dharma" Roeser, Sandy Pearlman)
The mission statement is clear from the opening chords of the first song, biker anthem 'Transmaniacon MC'. While the distorted guitar chords come crashing down in the intro as heavy as they come, they are not your regular Sabbath power chords. All sorts of strange things go on in Blue Öyster Cult's guitar riffs – substituted root notes and jazzy intervals. The effect is at once familiar and unsettling – the sound is that of British hard rock, but the notes are an amalgamation of psychedelia, jazz and prog rock. And when the drums come in, things are further confounded by Albert Bouchard's snappy, syncopated jazz feel. Then comes the Manzarek-esque organ, and then a

rock'n'roll piano! The surprises keep popping up even in the first few seconds of the song.

And yet, none of this cleverness can undermine the menacing, bone-crushing impact of the song. Eric Bloom, whose voice is so recognisable and confident even on this first album, delivers a litany of biker obscurantisms, half chanted, half whispered. His vocals carry echoes of expressive blues singers like Screamin' Jay Hawkins and British disciples like Arthur Brown and Eric Burdon, as well as obvious vocal hero Jim Morrison. But he adds to that an East Coast toughness, a kind of mean street credibility that is haunting and powerful. The lyrics, our very first introduction into Sandy Pearlman's *Imaginos* universe, are downright terrifying. How's this for an opening stanza?

> *With Satan's hog no pig at all*
> *And the weather's getting dry*
> *We'll head south from Altamont*
> *In a cold-blood traveled trance*
> *So clear the road, my bully boys*
> *And let some thunder pass*
> *We're pain, we're steel, a plot of knives*
> *We're Transmaniacon MC*

Only Sandy himself, rest his soul, knows exactly what it all means, but the Transmaniacon MC appear to be a very sinister MC club, possibly responsible for that end of the summer of love at the Altamont, possibly adoptive parents to the diabolical wunderkid from the stars, Imaginos (more on him later) himself ('The ghouls adopt that child/Whose name resounds forever'), and definitely heavily into drugs and violence ('reds and monocaine, yeah/pure nectar of antipathy'). Basically, a group of misfits you'd never want to meet, and Eric really lets you feel that in his delivery. Also of note here, as on the rest of the album, is a reverberant and almost soft-focus production that again, just like that jazzy touch, subverts the otherwise dark and foreboding nature of the music. Production-wise, the early BÖC albums are almost anti-Black Sabbath. Where the Sab's early albums were dry, brash, uncluttered and almost mono affairs, producers Sandy Pearlman and Murray Krugman, along with engineer David Lucas, wrapped the Cult's songs in a halo of plate reverbs, dampened highs and creative use of the stereo image.

'I'm On the Lamb But I Ain't No Sheep' (Bloom, A. Bouchard, Pearlman)

Just as you think you are beginning to figure out this disturbing psych-metal-jazz hybrid though, you're taken for another spin. Next up is the downright bizarre 'I'm On The Lamb But I Ain't No Sheep'. How's that for a title? It opens up with some very Southern rock-sounding plucked chords, mixed in typical early BÖC fashion with a dense reverb panned hard-right. The progression is basically borrowed from Captain Beefheart's 'Frying Pan'. The band picks up with a boogie-lite groove before Eric Bloom sings another set of Pearlman lyrics that actually surpass the previous song in their outlandishness. Images of Canadian mounted police are mashed up with S&M and arctic canines.

> *Got a whip in my hand, baby*
> *And a girl or a husky*
> *At the leather's end*

Musically the song is held down by Joe Bouchard's bass, a sort of walking boogie bass, while brother Albert does a high-tempo dance on his snare drum. Donald really shines on this track with some stellar country rock-inflected leads as well as some solid power chording. Interestingly, this song was attempted a couple of times in their pre-BÖC days, both as Oaxaca and as Stalk-Forrest Group. Both recordings can be found on *St. Cecilia: The Elektra Years*. And if that wasn't enough, the group would re-record this on their sophomore album, but more on that later.

'Then Came the Last Days of May' (Roeser)

Next up is one of the highlights of the band's entire catalogue, and in this author's opinion one of the finest rock ballads ever written. According to the band themselves it was largely on the merit of Donald's 'Then Came the Last Days of May' that the band got signed to Columbia, because label boss Clive Davis loved it so much. To this day this wistful song remains a fan favourite and a live staple. The song's influence extends far beyond the Cult: British '80s pop favourites Tears for Fears were famously formed after one half of the duo, Roland Orzabal, heard the other half of the duo, Curt Smith, sing along to 'Then Came the Last Days of May', which turned out to be a favourite song for both of them.

The song itself is an effervescent wonder of laid-back West Coast chords, gripping storytelling lyrics and achingly melodic guitar. The song starts with a hit on the snare, followed by that already trademark right-panned reverb. Actually, the snare drum is followed by a reverberating echo throughout the song, helping evoke the vast space of the desert where the story plays out. Then comes the crisp chord progression carried by the guitar and our first encounter with Donald's highly emotional, melodic lead mode. He spins out a beautiful, spectral melody that utilizes bluesy tricks like blue note bends without really sounding bluesy at all. As his finger slides off the final note of the first lead, we get another revelation: Donald's vocals. A boyish, airy voice, smooth as silk, reminding this author a bit of original Steely Dan lead singer David Palmer. With remarkable melodic sensibility, Donald relates a tale that is based on actual events: Three Long Island kids went on a dope-buying expedition in Arizona that ended tragically, with two of them shot to death. While the song is mellow and laid-back, it conveys all the melancholy and loneliness of the desolate Arizona landscape ('parched land, no desert sand/ the sun is just a dot'), while the guitar solos draw the dramatic arc and play out the tragedy. *AllMusic* writer Donald Guarisco describes it well in a review of the song: 'the melancholy sting of Dharma's electric guitar leads and touches of rattlesnake-sounding percussion hint at the tragedy to come and the song closes with a melancholy coda where ghostly wordless harmonies soar over stinging guitar lines.' 'Then Came the Last Days of May' would prove to be a pivotal Blue Öyster Cult moment, both in its own right and as an early warning of the power of Donald's pop sensibilities.

'Stairway to the Stars' (A. Bouchard, Roeser, Richard Meltzer)
The tempo picks up after this pensive number, for a bit of a boogie romp called 'Stairway to the Stars', not to be confused with the similarly titled Glenn Miller standard. Richard Meltzer, Sandy Pearlman's old college buddy, wrote the lyrics for this. Where Pearlman's lyrics tend to be a bit obtuse and esoteric, Meltzer operates in a more humoristic, surreal space. 'Stairway' is a bit of a cynical commentary on autograph writing and fan worship. Musically this is not the most remarkable BÖC song, but it's an energetic little rocker and has always served the band well live.

'Before the Kiss, a Redcap' (Allen Lanier, Murray Krugman, Roeser, Pearlman)
'Before the Kiss, a Redcap' is a song as fascinating as the title promises. It starts out as a bouncy rock'n'roll number sung by Donald, who proves just as adept at rocking material as the introspective stuff. The lyrics, another Pearlman classic, are multi-layered and mysterious. 'Redcap' refers to a drug, probably a red pill of some kind, and the kiss takes place at an actual haunt for the boys in the band, Conry's. There were two Conry's Bars, referred to as Conry's East and Conry's West, and Blue Öyster Cult played them both. There are possibly lesbian overtones here, a foreshadowing of the song 'Astronomy' that like 'Before the Kiss' deals with Suzy, an experimental lady if we are to believe the lyrics. There is a sort of Lynchian atmosphere to the proceedings – the barroom setting, the dark sexuality, the mystery and an undercurrent of danger.

> *Their lips apart like a swollen rose*
> *Their tongues extend, and then retract*
> *A redcap, a redcap, before the kiss, before the kiss.*

There are also hints of Pearlman's occult preoccupations. Martin Popoff refers to Sandy Pearlman explaining that 'The Motif of the Rose' was conceived as some kind of clandestine fascist organization working in the shadows. This all points forward to *Secret Treaties* and the occult origins of WWII. One thing that strikes the listener when it comes to Pearlman's lyrics is that even though the wilful obscurantism makes them difficult or even impossible to understand in a straightforward manner, they are peculiarly poetic and attractive all the same. There is a flow and a dark beauty to the words.

> Beware the limping cat
> Whose black teeth grip between loose jaws
> Still ripe and fully bloomed
> A rose that's not from anywhere
> That you would know or I would care

Another interesting aspect to the song is that midways through, it breaks into a jaunty jazz tune, complete with djangoesque chording from Donald and a great walking bass from Joe. These forays into jazz would pop up occasionally, perhaps most conspicuously in the *Cultösaurus Erectus* track 'Monsters' almost a decade later.

'Screams' (Joe Bouchard)

That brings us, if we're looking at it old school, to side B of the LP and a highlight on the record, Joe Bouchard's epic and angst-filled 'Screams'. This was a Joe song through and through, both lyrics and music written by him, and sung by him. Just like 'Last Days of May', it starts with Albert hitting his snare, and a reverb blossoming in its wake. Then comes a dense, claustrophobic arrangement, a hard rock/psychedelic hybrid bordering on progressive rock with a prominent bass and interesting processed keyboards behind the guitars. A wall of vocals, many of them heavily processed, present a languid, psychedelic melody that is seemingly at odds with the sinister lyrics.

> Screams in the night, sirens delight
> Heat, broken glass, Satan's bred trash

The fragmented presentation of a paranoia-inducing, broken cityscape reminds one of *Dhalgren*, sci-fi author Samuel R. Delany's classic exploration of future urbanity (a book that coincidentally features a character named Dragon Lady, just like the '80s Blue Öyster Cult tune). The song goes through many changes and switches in mood from the exotic and mysterious to sheer panic. There's also some very tasty electric piano playing from Allen Lanier on this, heavily treated with echoes that make the notes seem like they are bouncing between the concrete walls of high-rises.

'She's as Beautiful as a Foot' (A. Bouchard, Lanier, Meltzer)

In a very proggy move the song transitions via a drum flourish into the arabesque work-out that is 'She's as Beautiful as a Foot'. This is another surreal Meltzer lyric set to music by Albert and Allen. It's a gorgeous tune, and maybe the most overtly psychedelic number on the album. Albert's drums really drive this one, with exotic tom patterns and lots of ghost notes on the snare. It's a tribute to the album's production that though this song is even more reverb-drenched than the rest of the album, the song still has clarity. Eric's delivery of Meltzer's possibly fetishistic lyrics is almost evil-sounding, but not in an overt, heavy metal way. As for the words themselves, well:

She's as beautiful as a foot
She's as beautiful as a foot
She heard somebody say, the other day

Didn't believe it when he bit into her face
Didn't believe it when he bit into her face
It tasted just like a fallen arch

It's not really possible to comment meaningfully on Meltzer's rock poetry, suffice it to say that it works in context. The tune goes back a long way, to the Soft White Underbelly days, and you can really hear it in the acid-laced haze that hovers over this song. But in all its weirdness it manages to be a very enjoyable pop tune with an infectious refrain.

'Cities on Flame with Rock and Roll' (A. Bouchard, Roeser, Pearlman)

The smoke-filled atmosphere is shattered by a sharp, heavy riff that signals the arrival of Albert Bouchard's seminal moment on the album: 'Cities on Flame with Rock and Roll'. Infamously, that opening riff is borrowed rather unsubtly from Black Sabbath's 'The Wizard', and then appended with a bit off of King Crimson's '21st Century Schizoid Man' – a song that is also referenced in the frantic instrumental section of the song. But who cares really, when the result is so engaging. Most of the credit for the song's success and longevity must go to Albert's drumming, that is both hard-rocking and swinging at the same time. The syncopations bring it into what we would call breakbeat territory today, and it's almost unfathomable that no rap artists have sampled the groove yet.

Lyrically, this is Sandy Pearlman's call to arms for a rock'n'roll revolution, a brave new, chaotic world where 'Marshall will buoy, but Fender control'. Albert takes the lead vocal for the first time and delivers with gusto. The first verse is as iconic a BÖC lyric as you get:

My heart is black, and my lips are cold
Cities on flame with rock and roll
Three thousand guitars they seem to cry
My ears will melt, and then my eyes

Just as iconic are the song's instrumental breaks, further elaborating on the King Crimson influence, specifically from '21st Century Schizoid Man' with that post-bebop meets hard rock riff and virtuoso start/stop sections filled out with frantic drum fills and intense soloing from Donald with lots of bends and double-stops. The song ends on a crashing power-chord, and before the reverb tail dies we are brought into the next tune ...

'Workshop of the Telescopes' (Bloom, A. Bouchard, J. Bouchard, Lanier, Roeser, Pearlman)

This is perhaps the most quintessentially BÖC song on the album, the one that really points forward to the next two albums especially. A mid-tempo, semi-progressive affair, the verses are built around a descending progression of floaty, dreamy chords while Eric sounds vaguely menacing in his recitation of Pearlman's alchemical prescriptions. The entire drum kit is treated with a slap-back echo that gives the drums an urgent, and again slightly psychedelic feel. After somewhat heavier refrains Donald launches into a couple of great oriental-sounding solos that can be seen as precursors to his famous instrumental break in '(Don't Fear) The Reaper'. The lyrics are ripe with occult and alchemical imagery.

> *By Silverfish Imperatrix, whose incorrupted eye*
> *Sees through the charms of doctors and their wives*
> *By Salamander Drake and the power that was undine*
> *Rise to claim Saturn, ring and sky*
> *By those who see with their eyes closed*
> *You'll know me by my black telescope*

The undine is an elemental creature known from alchemical writings, and the salamander is another creature central to the art of alchemy. And to see with one's eyes closed is a concept that will recur as the story of *Imaginos* unfolds. Alchemical and esoteric concepts are regularly used by Pearlman, partly to describe the transformational processes that Imaginos the 'hero' goes through. In short, 'Workshop of the Telescopes' is a central song to the *Imaginos* cycle. It's also worth mentioning that this song appears in a phenomenal 1972 live version on the 4-track live EP that has sometimes been available as *The Bootleg EP* – this version eventually got included on the quintessential BÖC 'best of', the double set also entitled *Workshop of the Telescopes*. This performance really shows how mature they were as a live band already in their first years as Blue Öyster Cult.

'Redeemed' (A. Bouchard, Lanier, Harry Farcas, Pearlman)

After these lofty, conceptual heights we are brought back down to earth with a somewhat unusual but enjoyable Cult tune, 'Redeemed'. The main bulk of the song was written by an acquaintance of the band, Harry Farcas, and then fleshed out by Albert and Allen, yet again with an impenetrable Pearlman lyric, this time about one Sir Rastus Bear whose redemption came in the form of a song.

Redeemed good lord, from the ice and cold
Redeemed from the cell to which I've been thrown
Redeemed by virtue of a country song

And indeed, the song is a cheerful-sounding country rock song, perhaps influenced by the country phases of Cult favourites like The Byrds and The Grateful Dead. It's odd, but it seems strangely fitting as an uplifting and uncomplicated end to an otherwise dark and challenging record.

The impact of Blue Öyster Cult's weird and wonderful debut album was felt both in its own time and subsequently. The LP has had a significant influence on the entire rock scene, and cover versions of songs from the album include power metallers Iced Earth's 'Cities on Flame', Aussie punkers Radio Birdman's 'Transmaniacon MC', indie rockers Gumball's 'She's as Beautiful as a Foot' and Norwegian art popsters The Opium Cartel's 'Then Came the Last Days of May'.

Two album tracks have also appeared in video games, 'Transmaniacon MC' in *Rock Band* and 'Cities on Flame' in *Guitar Hero III*.

It's hard to imagine that Columbia thought at the time that such a subversive and genre-defying record could provide hit singles, but they did attempt a 45 with 'Cities on Flame with Rock and Roll'. It did not chart, but that of course did not stop it from becoming one of the band's most beloved tracks. The album itself accumulated acceptable sales over time, and after four months it did crack the Billboard 200, eventually climbing to a modestly respectable 172nd place.

More importantly, maybe especially to mastermind and rock critic Sandy Pearlman, the album was a critical success. Rolling Stone's Lester Bang liked the album and heaped lavish praise on songs like 'Cities on Flame' ('deep gutty guitar slices and triumphantly sociopathic lyrics') and 'Then Came the Last Days of May' ('a quietly ominous guitar solo … it's a teen tragedy of our time. Of such stuff are great songs made.').

In *The Village Voice*, Robert Christgau proclaimed: 'The tightest and most musical hard rock record since – dare I say it – *'Who's Next'*.'

And *Creem*, probably the hippest rock rag around at the time, were quoted in an ad for the album saying: 'Get behind the Blue Öyster Cult before they get behind you.' Sound advice, probably. *Creem* also named the band best new act of the year in 1972.

Other musicians also started noticing the Öyster boys as they were touring the album. Iggy Pop, whose Stooges supported Blue Öyster Cult on a 1973 gig (incidentally Kiss' debut concert as well), thought the band 'were like an estimable, intelligent, sort of precursors of Queensrÿche'. (Iggy Pop and Lars Ulrich, interview with *So What!*, April 26. 2017). Musicians who at the time were exposed to early Blue Öyster Cult and inspired by what they heard range from Ratt's Stephen Pearcy via The Minutemen's Mike Watt (who told punk website *Dementlieu*: 'I really loved that band') to Body Count's Ice T.

Chapter 3: Echoes of Empires
Tyranny and Mutation (Columbia 1973)

Personnel:
Eric Bloom: stun guitar, synthesisers, vocals
Donald "Buck Dharma" Roeser: guitar, vocals
Allen Lanier: keyboards, rhythm guitar
Joe Bouchard: bass guitar, keyboards, vocals
Albert Bouchard: drums, vocals
Produced at Columbia Studios, New York 1972 by Murray Krugman and Sandy Pearlman
Release date: February 1973
Highest chart places: 122 (US)
Running time: 38:11

The debut album catapulted the Öyster boys into the full-blown rock'n'roll circus. Intensive touring ensued, notably with Alice Cooper which turned out to be a real schooling in stagecraft. Joe Bouchard described the steep learning curve of early touring in an interview with *Classic Rock Revisited*:

> *We played with the Byrds... we did a tour of New England and Upstate New York, and it was a disaster. They just didn't want to hear our music. Our album wasn't even out yet, so nobody knew us. We were pretty awkward.*
>
> *We took some time off after the tour and we knew we had to get better. We went and saw this band called Alice Cooper - I saw them at the Academy of Music in New York City. It was a two o'clock in the morning show. There were four acts on the bill ... Dr. John and some others. Alice Cooper, as a band, was great. We knew we wanted to get as organised and tight as that band.*

Eric Bloom echoed the experience in an interview with *Falls Church News-Press*:

> *We were lucky enough to get on a tour with Alice Cooper and that's when we really started learning how the rock business worked. And we learned a lot working with him ... We sort of learned at his feet how to do a rock show. He was kind of our mentor. We really owe him a lot. I think that everyone learned how to do a rock show from him because he originated sort of the modern-day rock show. I would say that anyone who has any kind of theatrical rock show owes it all to him.*

As a result of this school of schlock rock, Blue Öyster Cult really found their feet as a live act, refining their image as leather-clad biker occultists. Eric Bloom claims to have worn sunglasses more or less constantly since he was 13, but the rest, the leather and the studs, came from Sandy Pearlman.

According to Bloom: 'He (Sandy) took me to a gay store in Manhattan and he said: 'This is where you buy leather clothes. They don't sell this stuff in Bloomingdales'. It seems pretty normal now, but not in 1971. I got my first outfit from Leatherman on Christopher Street. When I put that stuff on I felt like Batman; nothing gay about it. I just felt very transformed when I put the clothes on.' (interview with Loudersound.com)

It wasn't just their image that got upgraded and fine-tuned before their sophomore release. Their musicianship matured, and the live playing turned the band into an alchemical furnace – a group of flaming telepaths, so to speak. This made *Tyranny and Mutation* a tighter, faster and harder record than their debut.

'The Red & the Black' (Eric Bloom, Albert Bouchard, Sandy Pearlman)

This was clear from the very opening of the album. After some introductory Who-type windmill chords the band locks into a furiously fast groove and a hard rocking riff that sounds eerily familiar. That's because 'The Red & the Black' is something as audacious as a remake of a song from the previous album: 'I'm on the Lamb But I Ain't No Sheep'. The hazy country rock of the original version has been replaced by a sort of crypto-speed metal. Interestingly, this version may have been inspired not so much by their live experiences with Alice Cooper as those with the Mahavishnu Orchestra, a band the Öyster boys both admired and had felt a little humiliated by when they toured with them ('they blew us off stage', according to Albert (*Agents of Fortune*, Popoff)). Albert's drums definitely have that Billy Cobham whirlwind quality, again mixing hard rock and jazz grooves in a way only Albert Bouchard can, a spirit-meeting of Gene Krupa and John Bonham. While 'The Lamb' had been a bit of a live failure because of its multi-part structure and laidback tempo, the double-time assault of *The Red & the Black* turned out to be a perfect concert opener on subsequent tours. The song ends with resplendent harmony lead guitars before an abrupt transition with a distorted synthesiser brings us to the boogie romp of …

'O.D.'d on Life Itself' (Bloom, A. Bouchard, Joe Bouchard, Pearlman)

The tempo is taken down a bit and the guitars roll along with a swampy feel while the organ joins and a Motown bass-line underpins proceedings. Eric Bloom is back in his low-key sinister mode, with especially the verses harbouring a quiet intensity worthy of Bloom's vocal idol Eric Burdon. This is a Sandy Pearlman-penned lyric. It's a little unclear if it ties directly in with the *Imaginos* concept, but it certainly has that cryptic poetic quality.

Writings appear on the wall
The curtains part and landscape fall
There, the writing's done, in blood
Like a mummy's inscription and a bat-wing tongue

Midways through the song we get a soaring, melodic Buck solo before the song returns to its swampy thump. A bit like 'Stairway to the Stars' on the first album, this is not the Cult's strongest musical number but it's fun and it works well in the context.

'Hot Rails to Hell' (J. Bouchard)

After the breathing space of 'O.D.'d', it's back into the furious up-tempo riffage with Joe Bouchard's classic 'Hot Rails to Hell', a definite highlight on the album. Less progressive than many of Joe's tunes, 'Hot Rails' is pure, blues-infused hard rock led by Joe's energetic lead vocals delivering another urban angst lyric. Partly inspired by real events, it was also an exposition on Joe's fascination with downtown New York.

Joe:

'Hot Rails to Hell' was one of those things where I wanted to write an up-tempo rock song. It is also kind of a story of an agent that we had, named Phil King, who came to an untimely end. I used to live with Phil. He got murdered over some gambling debts. He was our agent and promoter in the early days.

I was hanging out with the guy who did the album cover, Bill Gawlik. We took the subway because he was too cheap to pay for a parking space in New York. We would drive to Queens and then we would get on the subway and go to New York. We went to a jazz concert in the city and then we took the subway back to Queens. On the way back to Queens, on the subway, the whole idea for 'Hot Rails to Hell' came to me. The guys liked it and it was the right song for our second album. It was put out as a single. It is a great song and it has survived the test of time.

(Interview with *Classic Rock Revisited*)

Brother Albert has memories of a challenging session for *Hot Rails to Hell*:
We did a few takes of 'Hot Rails to Hell.' After the take that ended up being on the record was done, Murray said 'Well, I like the guitar parts, I like the whole track, but some of those drum tracks I don't like, so why don't you overdub the drums?' I said, 'Oh ... well can I listen to my old drum part and put a new part in?' and he said 'No, we took eight tracks, we can't do that, you'll have to just listen to the guitar.' No reference! They said, 'Listen, if this doesn't work, the track's no good. You'll have to do it over again anyway. Why don't you try it?' So I did. One take. That's the first time I tried it and they said, 'Fine ... That's good, that's what we want.' I said 'You're kidding!' They said 'No! It's good! listen!' I mean, if

you listen to it you can hear it that it's overdubbed. It's not exactly tight all the time, but it's kind of funny. That's the first and the only time on a Blue Öyster Cult album that I've overdubbed drums. With Tom Werman, he had me punching in drums sometimes. As far as replacing the entire drum track, that's the only time that I can remember doing that. It still blows my mind when I hear it, like wow I can't believe I actually did that! That was pretty weird. Although on the other hand it's just a testament to how steady Donald can play. That he really had an even keel rhythmically, and that I really did play to Donald's rhythm guitar part.
(*Morning Final* #10).

And it's a testament to Joe's strength as a writer that this tune has survived in the band's live sets to this day.

Towards the end of the song Donald launches into an aggressive quickfire guitar solo before the vocals come back in for an ending that references the band's love of surf rock, both with Donald's Dick Dale-style guitar effects and the Beach Boys harmony vocals. The ending riff runs through a filter that gradually removes the lower frequencies until just a thin, AM radio sound is left and is replaced by the opening riff of side A's last track.

'7 Screaming Diz-Busters' (A. Bouchard, J. Bouchard, Donald Roeser, Pearlman)

'7 Screaming Diz-Busters' is a bit of a personal favourite for this writer, a sprawling, dark epic that moves through many sections and takes the listener on a journey through the inner circles of hell. The song is a group composition, augmented by some of Pearlman's most mystifying and beautiful poetry.

Bury me near the secret cave
So they'll not know the way
Bury me there behind the rose
So they'll not rile my grave
I'll not reveal whose name's still lost

Joe Bouchard had a lot of writing input and also rearranged the lyrics to make them more singable.

'7 Screaming Diz-busters' was a lot of fun. Basically what I did I had laid out, even though everybody had contributed their various riffs and parts to the song, I had ripped apart Sandy's original lyric to make it a bit more musical and lyrical. I just got up one morning, and went down to the Hammond organ, we had a big Hammond organ in the living room, and started playing, 'they held their heads with laughs of pain,' and most of it came out pretty good. I guess I was sort of influenced by the

Allman Brothers on the opening riff but other than that it was sort of like this gothic thing, and we had this good piece of a song that was going to happen. (Morning Final #10)

There are so many things that deserve mention in the song, from the adventurous and diabolic use of harmony (no doubt creditable to Joe's background on classical piano) to Eric's theatrical and bone-chilling Luciferian chanting. Albert is in his most progressive mode here, ripping through the many changes while stile keeping an almost motorik sense of propulsion throughout. Allen's bubbling, gothic organ is also of note, adding a bit of vintage horror movie atmosphere to the proceedings. Then there is again the tempo, which at times is frighteningly high. Sandy himself proudly proclaimed the song the precursor to speed metal, maybe not entirely unjustified.

'Baby Ice Dog' (Bloom, A. Bouchard, Patti Smith)

On to side B. There has been some controversy among fans about the 'The Black' (the album's sides are designated as 'The Red' (side A) and 'The Black' (side B) on the sleeve). Some feel it is a let-down after the heaviness of 'The Red'. And it's true, there is a much lighter feel to some of the songs on side B, but to this author's ears that is one of the strengths of the album – there is light and shade, humour and danger.

The lightness is felt in 'The Black''s first track, Bouchard and Bloom's 'Baby Ice Dog'. Musically it's a very strong statement, a mash-up of pop melody and guitar crunch with catchy hooks and a jaunty rhythm. Lyrically, it is very, very strange. This was Blue Öyster Cult's first lyrical collaboration with Patti Smith, who had been introduced to the band by Richard Meltzer, and who had given several lyrics to Albert to see if he could put music to them. This was before she herself became a recording artist. 'Baby Ice Dog' was one that Albert felt he could work with, musically. The text is downright disturbing in its murky sexuality. Some read it as a lesbian tale while others see bestiality.

They'd like to make it
With my big black dog
But they just don't know how to ask
You know they'd like to try
Anything that comes into their minds

Maybe the black dog is the one we hear howling at the beginning and end of the song?

After the first vocal sections the song breaks down into a sort of 'Fever' segment with minimal accompaniment, some moody guitar from Buck and a little blues chant from Eric. Later in the song we get rollicking piano and some nice rock'n'roll organ from Allen. All in all a short but sweet demonstration of the Cult's poppier side.

'Wings Wetted Down' (A. Bouchard, J. Bouchard)

After the black dog stops howling we are introduced to the most sinister opening riff on the album. 'Wings Wetted Down' is the most overtly gothic tune here, sounding like a sophisticated, progged up Black Sabbath. Albert's toms resound like thunder while the guitars go to all those eerie places Tony Iommi loves. It's mostly a Joe song, which explains the harmonic sophistication.

> *I have to confess several of the words were 'freely' adapted from Spanish poet Pablo Neruda. Just a line here or there. It was an English translation I was reading at the time. But it was no more than John Lennon's borrowing a line from Kahlil Gibran.*
> (hotrails.co.uk)

It's texturally interesting, because while the electric guitars get quite heavy, the verses are carried by an airy acoustic guitar and a bouncy bass. Donald delivers one of his finest solos on the album here, a double-tracked affair that is restrained and melodic and treated to a psychedelic Leslie effect.

Joe has pointed out that while the lyrics reek of a Transylvanian atmosphere, he does not actually sing 'echoes of vampires', as most listeners have thought. It actually goes:

> *The voices sound deadly*
> *Sometimes I hear*
> *Echoes of empires*
> *Spread throughout the sky*

The song ends with a slow blues lick from Donald and the sound of a draining sink, for reasons unknown.

'Teen Archer' (Bloom, Roeser, Richard Meltzer)

Without pause we are taken into the next tune, probably the poppiest, some would say silliest, on the album. To this author's ears 'Teen Archer' is another one of the highlights of the album, a fine display of Donald's pop sensibilities and a great opportunity for the band to show its lighter touch. The song is built around another fast tempo and a tight rhythm from Albert. The guitar riffs are actually quite heavy, but Donald's boyish vocals and the playful melody subvert any real heaviness and turn the song into one of the earliest examples of what would later be called pop metal. It's easy to imagine that Ratt, for instance, learnt a lot from this tune. Midways through, it gets a little proggy, first with a solo from Donald introduced by some fierce tremolo picking, and then a solo spot for Allen, who rips a great organ solo before switching to some bluesy electric piano. There's even a short drum flourish from Albert. The verses return with a slight shift in rhythmic and harmonic emphasis, lending the melody even more energy and urgency – a neat trick. The lyrics for this song are by Richard Meltzer, which means that we may expect some surreal but poetic nonsense. Gordon Fletcher, in his *Rolling Stone* review of the album called the song 'a passionate tale of adolescent sex orgies and the distribution of wealth'. You could see why:

She got more than you or I, she got more than me
She got more than you or I, she got more than me
She get, she get wild, she gets wild
Balling all night balling all day, she won't ball on me
Balling all night balling all day, she won't ball on me
She will, she will die, she will die, she don't care

'Mistress of the Salmon Salt (Quicklime Girl)' (A. Bouchard, Pearlman)

After such merry-making it's time to get serious again at album's end. Well, almost, anyway. Because a title like 'Mistress of the Salmon Salt (Quicklime Girl)' doesn't exactly signal a serious subject matter. And yet, the song starts on a very dark note, with a doom-laden riff before the subdued verse melody with its undercurrent of menace begins. This is an Albert Bouchard-penned tune, which typically implies a lot of contrasting between heavier and lighter sections. This is no exception. The chorus is a classic Cult move in that it combines a hard-rocking blues riff with heavenly, Byrds-like vocal harmonies. After the second chorus the song breaks down into an interesting section with horror movie-like minor progressions and darkly chanted lyrics from Eric.

A harvest of life a harvest of death
One body of life one body of death
And when you've gone and choked to death
With laughter and a little step
I'll prepare the quicklime, friend
For your ripe and ready grave
For your ripe and ready grave

Pearlman's lyrics for 'Mistress' centre around themes of fertility, death and harvest time, maybe a nod to the myth of Demeter and Persephone. And the sinister dressing-up of the theme reminds one of Stephen King's brilliant short story *Children of the Corn*, first published in 1977 and later turned into a film. Knowing what a big BÖC fan King is, who knows if some inspiration may have seeped into his writing from this song?

But back to the music. Allen Lanier grabs another few seconds in the spotlight with a cool, 'Riders on the Storm' style organ solo before Donald launches into a tense and precise guitar lead. At the very end of the song the 'harvest chant' recurs in an even more intense and slightly chaotic manner.

All in all, this is a very worthy ending to one of the seminal albums in the

Cult's career. 'Mistress' combines the band's Sabbath ambitions with exactly the kind of dark romanticism that would catapult the band into stardom when '(Don't Fear) The Reaper' hit the radio-waves a few years later.

For *Tyranny and Mutation* the band chose to work just with Sandy Pearlman and Murray Krugman in the studio, leaving producer/engineer David Lucas temporarily out of the picture. This was a bit of a shame, because while the band had gotten better, the production suffers a bit compared to the debut album. On the upside there's a subtler reverb use here, which gives the album that harder edge that the boys had probably wanted from the start. There is a rawer, more direct quality to the proceedings. But the album is sorely lacking in bass, making the songs sound thinner and more anaemic than they deserve. There's also less of the wide-screen stereo experience that the previous album offered. Thankfully Lucas returned for the much better sounding *Secret Treaties*.

Another cause for the somewhat unfinished feel of the production could be the band's hectic touring schedule, which left little time for actual studio work. According to Eric Bloom, 'The second we were ready with the material, we were shuffled into the studio to produce. And then we had to get back on the road so that we could eat.' (Interview with *Musicradar*)

The somewhat lacklustre production didn't really get in the way of the impact of the songs though, something that showed in sales. In three months the album climbed 40 places higher than the debut, landing at 122 in the Billboard charts. Again, critics were enthusiastic, with the above-mentioned *Rolling Stone* review concluding the album was 'one molten hook after another', while the *Village Voice's* Robert Christgau claimed the band 'impales the entire heavy ethos on a finely-honed guitar neck'.

Tyranny and Mutation was the second and last album to feature the iconic artwork of the mysterious Gawlik, something that deserves special mention. Very little is known about William 'Bill' Gawlik beyond his time as an associate of the Öyster boys. Early Soft White Underbelly member John Wiesenthal had made the initial contact with the enigmatic artist.

> Bill Gawlik! I brought him in! He was a crazy design student who'd dropped out of Parsons School of Design. He'd been a student of William Katavalos and was exploding with ideas about cosmology, WWII, social transformation. He was an insomniac and we'd stay up all night filling up rolls of butcher paper with magic marker diagrams.
> (hotrailstohell.co.uk)

The story differs somewhat regarding where exactly he studied, and what. Some, like John, have him as a design student. Others remember him as an architecture student (William Katavalos was an architecture professor), and Sandy Pearlman has described him on several occasions as a latter-day Albert Speer (Hitler's monument-building architect). What we do know is that he attended Stony Brook University for a while, and that is presumably where he met John Wiesenthal and later, Sandy Pearlman.

The story goes that Sandy almost literally bumped into Gawlik at the university grounds at Stony Brook and got to see a roll of butcher paper that was filled with Gawlik's architectural sketches. Gawlik rolled out the whole scroll for Sandy to see, and legend has it that it stretched the length of the main campus building. Gawlik described the sketches as his vision for a future America, again apparently inspired by Albert Speer. Sandy understood that he had something special here, and eventually secured a budget of $500 to commission Gawlik to make the first BÖC cover. It is unclear whether he actually moved into the famous band house, or just was a frequent visitor. Eric Bloom remembers that 'He was sort of a unique and eccentric artist. He had blueprints for full size exoskeletons that people could wear. He had really unusual drawings of robots and all kinds of different line drawings. He seemed like a natural to lend us artwork for the first album cover (…) We had a band house in '71-'72 and Gawlick (sic) almost moved in with me but it didn't quite work out.' (Interview with *Classic Rock Revisited*)

Either way, Gawlik did make that first album cover, and both Sandy and the boys were very happy with it.

When it came time for album no. 2, Gawlik had left Stony Brook and was renting a space in a garret where he couldn't afford heat. He was making a scarce living as a taxi driver in NY when Sandy reconnected with him and made him another $500 offer for a new cover. As the story goes, it was a torturous process to get Gawlik to finish the new cover on time. By all accounts he was not the most stable of persons. '(He) drove a taxi in the city and had a machete underneath his seat. True', says Joe (hotrailstohell.co.uk), while Sandy at one time mused: 'when *Taxi Driver* came out, I really thought that Scorsese must have ridden around with Bill Gawlik, you know, talked to him and got the idea for the film from him!' (*Agents of Fortune*, Popoff)

So, freezing in his garret, feeling slightly paranoid and brewing on esoteric cosmologies, he tried to finish the drawing while listening to the first Blue Öyster Cult album over and over. Allegedly, just before he handed over the artwork to Sandy, barely in the nick of time, he told him something to the effect of 'listening to that album is like tyranny and mutation', and that's where the album title came from.

And as if two album covers and a title weren't enough, the mysterious Gawlik also bequeathed another precious gift to the band: The 'Chronos' logo.

It was Gawlik's own idea to add the symbol to the first album cover, as a bit of an afterthought. The symbol does bear a striking resemblance to the astrological symbol of the mythological Greek titan Chronos, reflected in later Roman mythology as Saturn. The original symbol combines a scythe with a cross-like form. The scythe was associated with Chronos since he was the Father of Time and thus associated with the harvest and the cycles of nature. The sickle, again with the cross at the end, was also the symbol of Ceres,

Goddess of the Harvest. This all brings us back to the recurring themes of harvest/reaper/death in the Cult's oeuvre, from 'Mistress of the Salmon Salt' via '(Don't Fear) The Reaper' to Donald's 'Harvest Moon'. Gawlik's modification of the symbol made it appear as an inverted question mark slashed by a cross-bar. It was such a striking and mysterious image that the band immediately decided to adopt it as their own symbol. Now, just to take things to their natural, esoteric conclusion, Chronos/Saturn is also associated with lead in astrology and alchemy, and lead is, as we know, a heavy metal. So there you go.

Chapter 4: Forest keys and whirlwind cold
Secret Treaties (Columbia 1974)
Personnel:
Eric Bloom: vocals, stun guitar, keyboards
Donald "Buck Dharma" Roeser: lead guitar, vocals
Allen Lanier: keyboards, rhythm guitar, synthesisers
Joe Bouchard: bass, vocals
Albert Bouchard: drums, vocals
Produced at CBS Studios, New York 1974 by Sandy Pearlman and Murray Krugman
Release date: April 1974
Highest chart places: 53 (US)
Running time: 38:35

Most Blue Öyster Cult aficionados would agree that this is where it all came together for the band. So many things were right about this album. The production is really strong – meaty and full, unlike *Tyranny*, and still with that whiff of psychedelia and The Doors that was introduced on the first album. The rhythms come at you like a juggernaut, the guitars are visceral and the vocals upfront. Apropos vocals, this is very much an Eric Bloom album, both in terms of his maturation as a singer and his contributions as a songwriter.

'This is my personal favourite. We had a band house in Eaton's Neck, New York. I lived there by myself. By this point, everybody else had their own apartments or lived with girlfriends, so when the band left, I'd be there with all the guitars and equipment. I would work on ideas and tunes, some of which became songs like 'ME 262'', Eric said told Musicradar of the experience. It wasn't just Eric who felt there was some extra breathing space to make *Secret Treaties*. The whole band and their producers had learnt a lesson with the hastily recorded *Tyranny and Mutation*, and took their time both to write, arrange, produce and record the material. And thankfully David Lucas was back in place as co-producer.

The original working title was 'Power in the Hands of Fools', tying in with Sandy's 'occult roots of WWII' theme which is fully explored on this album. They landed on the simpler and snappier *Secret Treaties* in the end. The WWII theme was explored specifically in Eric's 'ME 262' and also in the originally unreleased track 'Boorman The Chauffeur', but the whole album reeks of a sinister, occult and aggressive atmosphere that I suspect Sandy and the boys had been chasing since the beginning.

'Career of Evil' (A. Bouchard, Patti Smith)
The show starts with a bang with Albert's 'Career of Evil', setting music to a Patti Smith poem originally titled 'Poem of Isadore Ducasse'. The opening riff is instantly memorable, and Allen's organ bubbling away finally has the body and definition it has deserved all along – it becomes an equal instrument

to the others rather than a vague embellishment. The fullness and breadth of the sound image is on a whole different level than the two previous albums. The bass really fills out the bottom range, the snare has real meat to it. And songwriting and arrangement-wise the boys had hit their stride at this point. There are simple touches that do so much, one example being in the pre-chorus of 'Career of Evil' where the band drops out, and only the drums remain to support Eric's exclamation that he 'will not apologise', making that line stand out starkly and effectively. Vocally this is also a very strong statement from Eric. The melody is minimalistic, and Eric's delivery is restrained and completely lacking in histrionics. Instead he manages to convey an impression of barely contained menace and aggression, held back only by extreme self-control. The effect is chilling. Especially coupled with Patti Smith's controversial lyrics.

> *I plot your rubric scarab*
> *I steal your satellite*
> *I want your wife to be my*
> *Baby tonight, baby tonight*
>
> *I choose to steal what you choose to show*
> *And you know I will not apologise*
> *You're mine for the taking*
>
> *I'm making a career of evil*

'Subhuman' (Bloom, Pearlman)

Typical of the insistent flow of this album, there is no pause before a bass note introduces the next song, Eric's beautiful and mysterious 'Subhuman'. This song really shows Eric's confidence as a songwriter. The opening is very striking, establishing the verses' characteristic pedal point bass in D, overlaid by tremoloed, suspended guitar chords. The moving chords and the static bass create a push & pull effect, a sense of unresolved tension that goes well with Sandy's convoluted lyrics.

> *I am becalmed*
> *Lost to nothing*
> *Warm weather and*
> *Holocaust*
>
> *Left to die by two good friends*
> *Abandoned me and put to sleep*
> *Left to die by two good friends*
> *Tears of God flow as I bleed*

'Subhuman', which was originally called 'Blue Öyster Cult' and reappeared under that name on *Imaginos* (more on that later in the book) is a very central chapter in the *Imaginos* saga, telling the story of our hero Imaginos as he is put to some kind of test ('left to die') and then rescued by strange denizens of the deep (the 'oyster boys' that enter later in the lyric).

The song picks up its pace in the chorus, which is introduced by a staccato two-note riff and some wonderfully syncopated drumming from Albert. The vocal sections of the song bookend a rather extraordinary solo from Donald, switching into a moody Robby Krieger mode with long, sustained notes and a laidback feel while Joe lays down a very Doors-like bass line underneath. There is in general a strong Doors vibe to the track, and especially a whiff of 'Riders on the Storm'.

'Dominance and Submission' (Bloom, A. Bouchard, Pearlman)

A ticking clock transports us from the calm before the storm of 'Subhuman' to the onslaught of 'Dominance and Submission', one the band's biggest live favourites.

'Dominance and Submission' is, like the best of the Cult's tunes, quite deceptive. After hearing it you're left with the impression of having experienced a very heavy and brutal song, but as a matter of fact the musical elements are mostly pop-leaning. The main riff, written by Eric, is a relatively cheerful chord ascension, and the vocal melody has a bit of The Animals' blues-pop in it. But the crunch of the double-tracked guitars, and the mischievous vocal delivery by Albert, gives a much darker impression than what the music actually implies. Of note is also Albert's 8th note kick drum that propels the song like a runaway locomotive. But of course, the highlight of the song is the call & response section, where 'dominance' and 'submission' compete with each other into ever heightening tension that is then released in Donald's absolutely furious and frenzied guitar solo. In live renditions this section would expand and build further, but on the album it ends with a psychedelic, pulsing synthesiser. But before that, a word on the lyrics.

According to the premier Cultologist, Bolle Gregmar, "Dominance and Submission' was the true story of an automobile ride taken with Suzy and her brother, in which some unexpected sexual actions were suggested.' (*Morning Final* #12). The lyrics were, not surprisingly, written by Sandy Pearlman, and while they don't seem to tie in with the *Imaginos* myth in any obvious way, they do deal with Sandy's pre-occupation with the revolutionary potential of rock'n'roll, previously explored in 'Transmaniacon MC' and 'Cities on Flame'.

Yeah, the radio was on – can't you dig the locomotion
Kingdoms of the radio, 45 RPM
Too much revolution, then

So far, so good, seems like a song about the '60s rock revolution, and they're driving around listening to singles on the radio. But then things get kinky, so to speak.

> Each night the covers were unfolded
> Each night it's Suzy's turn to ride
> While Charles, the one they call her brother
> Covers on his eyes
> Murmurs in the background
> It will be time

What exactly is going on in this song? Add to this the thump and grind of the 'dominance – submission' section and it all seems very dubious. Yet in a 1975 interview with *The NME* Sandy himself skipped the sexual part and talked about the revolutionary aspects:

> In 1963 I was being driven back from a New Year's Eve party when The Beatles came over the airwaves for the first time. It seemed so revolutionary in terms of consciousness that what is represented was a new factor in mass culture and '63 was the watershed. The song reflects the parallelism between revolutionary consciousness in the mass and how it affects the individual. The sublimated heat of rock 'n' roll, so, long suppressed, and driven underground, was being revealed and no one could stop it. (NME, 1975)

So, who knows. Maybe the incident with Charles and his sister is something Sandy would rather keep private ...

'ME 262' (Bloom, Roeser, Pearlman)

The song ends with the previously mentioned synthesiser oscillating away until the relentless boogie riffing of 'ME 262' kicks in. The main riff is another of Eric Bloom's creations from his days as the only inhabitant in the band house – evidently a very creative period for him.

> I lived in the band house - I was the only one that lived there. It had an upright piano in the living room, and just sat down at the piano, had that lyric there, and I just sort of banged that out. I can't remember what the inspiration was, but I put my hands down and that's what came out. (Interview with Songfacts)

Musical embellishments from Donald, and lyrics again from Sandy.

To give a little background, the Messerschmidt ME 262 was the world's first fighter jet, developed by the Germans during WWII. It didn't become properly operational until the end of the war, which meant that even though it was a very effective plane and weapon, it had negligible impact on the war. Had they finished the plane sooner, it might have prolonged the war considerably. As it was, the plane had several successful missions in 1944 and '45. It was faster than any plane the Allied forces had, and easy to navigate at high speeds. It was also equipped with the formidable R4M missile which, when it hit home, did a lot of damage. US and UK forces soon realised that you couldn't compete with the 'Stormbird' as the Germans called it, in air-to-air combat, so the only way to counter it was by hitting it on land or during take-off or landing. Blue Öyster Cult's song narrates a tale from the perspective of a German pilot during a raid on British bombers in April 1945, at the very end of the war. It is unclear whether 'Captain Von Ondine' (again, an alchemical reference there) is the actual pilot or the one ordering the raid, but anyway it appears to be successful, if dramatic.

In a G-load disaster from the rate of climb
Sometimes I'd faint and be lost to our side
But there's no reward for failure – but death
So watch me in mirrors keep me on the glidepath

Get me through these radars, no, I cannot fail
While my great silver slugs are eager to feed
I can't fail – No, not now
When twenty five bombers wait ripe

They hung there dependent from the sky
Like some heavy metal fruit
These bombers are ripe and ready to tilt
Must these Englishmen live that I might die
Must they live that I might die

Clearly these lyrics are part of the *Imaginos* cycle, dealing again with WWII as an occult or alchemical/transformational event. But this time it is told in the form of a little personal vignette, making the meaning clearer and the impact greater. The historical correctness of the lyrics is somewhat questionable, however. Most of the raids carried out by the Stormbirds this late in the war were on Soviet targets rather than British ones. But then again, Sandy has made it very clear that *Imaginos* refers to an alternate history or reality, so we'll let that pass.

Musically the song is carried by Eric's strong boogie riffs, imparting a Southern flavour to the song. A cool break occurs for the 'they hung there dependent from the sky/like some heavy metal fruit' section, where Albert switches to his toms for some nice, pattern-based drumming. The verses have a call & response feel to them, with the first parts sung by what sounds like the whole band, and the following phrase sung by Eric alone, and so forth. There's also a tongue-in-cheek doo-wop backing vocal buried in the mix in the later part of the verse. Around the middle of the song a new riff enters, a bit more subdued, accompanied by the sound of a legion of marching, German boots, air sirens and exploding bombs, a theatrical, dramatic break of the kind they would repeat in songs like 'Black Blade' and 'Joan Crawford' later in their career. The song then returns to its regular groove with heightened intensity, Eric sounding as possessed and driven as he ever has before the song ends in an inferno of sirens and sound. 'ME 262' is one of the rawest, most visceral songs in Blue Öyster Cult's discography and an impressive end to side A of the album.

'Cagey Cretins' (A. Bouchard, Richard Meltzer)
Side B starts off with two Meltzer-penned lyrics, the first of which is 'Cagey Cretins'. The words make very little sense, even by Meltzer standards, but they're certainly entertaining, and according to Albert, who wrote the music, the song is about a serial killer. That reading has some plausibility.

> *Dumb clouds are ringing*
> *Ringing in my ear*
> *Mother's wombs are crying*
> *Ringing in my fear*
> *Mothers never run*
> *Except when rape is near*
> *Ooo cagey*

What's certain is that the words invoke the same kind of semi-comical discomfort that all of Meltzer's lyrics do – there's a joke in there somewhere, and it's probably on you, the listener. In that respect, early Blue Öyster Cult had a lot in common with Steely Dan, a band we know had some influence on BÖC in the mid-70s. Both bands were built around a core of East Coast college hang-arounds with equally smart-ass attitudes and dry-witted senses of humour, so similarities are not surprising.

For 'Cagey Cretins' Albert reached back into the band's history and borrowed a small riff from an otherwise unremarkable Soft White Underbelly track called 'Bark in the Sun'. Out of that he built a tense and muscular little tune that, while being one of the less extraordinary songs on the record, still works well in context and gives quite a chilling introduction to side B. The song features some tasty organ work from Allen and a section that sounds like a sped-up version of Pink Floyd's 'Set the Controls for the Heart of the Sun'.

'Harvester of Eyes' (Bloom, Roeser, Meltzer)
Without missing a beat, we transition into the thudding steamroller beat of 'Harvester of Eyes'. The introduction of this tune is a testament to the production prowess of the Pearlman/Krugman/Lucas team at this point. The song starts with the central riff, a metalised blues hybrid, in the left channel,

swiftly followed by a muted, staccato single note in the opposite channel while an organ starts swelling back in the left channel. The staccato guitar crescendos into a complementary riff to the main riff, and then we roll along with the full band, with what sounds like a piano craftily tucked behind the guitar in the right channel to fill out the sound. It's touches like these, that are basically inaudible to the casual listener but that do so much for the overall sound, that help ensure the longevity of certain Cult albums as audiophile objets de désir.

The song has the same swampy feeling we experienced on the first album, with Eric intoning the lyrics like a voodoo priest. His vocals here are a definite highlight on the album. Adding to the New Orleans/Dr. John atmosphere is Allen's boogie-woogie piano – buried a tad too deep in the mix, unfortunately. Around the one-and-a-half-minute mark we get another nice arrangement touch, when the whole band drops out, leaving a single, thumping guitar in the left channel pumping away until a sinister but melodic riff enters on the right. Cue guitar solo, one of Donald's most impassioned on the album replete with double-stops and blue note bends while Albert seems to dance around on the cymbals. It's rare to hear such hard rocking music played with such elegance. Back to the vocal section, augmented by some haunting, half-whispered backing vocals reciting the songs title. And then a complete break, and one of the proggier moments on the album. Some furiously played guitar introduces a jazzy drum and bass groove with some very demonic and tortured sounding guitar progressions over it and Eric doing some outlandish, semi-scatting vocals that remind this writer of Boz Burrell's improvised vocals on King Crimson's live *Earthbound* record from 1972. During the short time this coda lasts one is ready to see Bela Lugosi come dancing out of the mist on some Haitian graveyard …

Interestingly, though, the lyrics do not deal with voodoo and black magic, but organ theft. The harvester of eyes appears to be some kind of psycho who gets off on stealing people's eyes.

I'm the eyeman of TV
With my ocular TB
I need all the peepers I can find
Inside the barn where you find the hay

Just last week I took a ride
So high on eyes I almost lost my way
I'm the Harvester of Eyes

The coda section elucidates the harvester's method, stalking the night looking for victims. This part was ad-libbed on the spot by Eric.

Again, there is no pause between tracks – the song climaxes and then subsides into a nursery rhyme melody played on what sounds like a music box. The little waltz has not been positively identified. Some argue it is an excerpt from the old waltz melody Donauwelle (Waves of the Donau), but there is dissent on the matter. Regardless, it is a very effective transition into what is essentially the beginning of the album's climax – the twin epics of 'Flaming Telepaths' and 'Astronomy'.

'Flaming Telepaths' (Bloom, A. Bouchard, Roeser, Pearlman)

Both of the closing songs on *Secret Treaties* are among the finest Blue Öyster Cult have ever written. Of the monumental, swirling 'Flaming Telepaths', Eric has said:

> *'Flaming Telepaths' was written I believe in either Eatons Neck or Dix Hills, en masse, in a collaborative fashion with all the band members in a room. I can't remember who came up with the germ of the idea, but when it came to creating the melody, I said, 'I think it should go this way,' and somebody said, 'It should go that way.' That's how all the credits came out. Sandy Pearlman wrote the lyric – it's one of those sci-fi impenetrable lyrics. He had a lot of influence from Lovecraft and a variety of sci-fi and fantasy influences.'*

Eric co-wrote the song with Albert and Donald. It starts in whirlwind fashion, hectic drums, swirling cymbals, a dramatic descending riff doubled by a moog synthesiser – it's a definitive, progressive hard rock statement. The insistent one-chord piano-pounding on top of the descending chords adds to the epic feel of the song. Once the verse enters, it turns out to be a long one, winding its way through myriad chords while building its way to the cryptic and anthemic chorus. Lyrically we are introduced again to one of Sandy's favourite themes, alchemy.

> *Experiments that failed too many times*
> *Transformations that were too hard to find*
> *Poisons in my bloodstream*
> *Poisons in my pride*
> *I'm after rebellion*
> *I'll settle for lies*

> *Yes I know the secrets of the iron and mind*
> *They're trinity acts, a mineral fire*
> *Yes I know the secrets of the circuitry mind*
> *It's a flaming wonder telepath*

Some people read the song mostly as a tale of addiction, but knowing Sandy's obsessions, the correct interpretation here is more likely the story of a mad scientist-type alchemist trying out potions on himself, searching for the ultimate elixir to open the gates of perception. Something that will turn him into a flaming wonder telepath. Echoes of the same theme can be found on the album *Imaginos* in the tune 'The Siege and Investiture of Baron Von Frankenstein's Castle at Weisseria', where they sing of 'The starry wisdom/Owned by the Baron/And he's got the cure/A drug by the name of World without end'. Clearly this is a narrative dealing with an alchemist's Promethean hubris.

The aforementioned moog synthesiser adds a new textural element to the Cult sound in this song, and it complements the 'science gone too far' aspect of the lyrics well. And there is more: After the second verse and chorus we get something entirely new in the Cult's toolbox; a synthesiser solo. With melodic grace and a good understanding of the strengths of the instrument, Allen weaves a smooth little solo melody on the moog before switching to a brief piano solo as well. It's amazing how much colour and textural interest those few seconds of synth add to the song. Donald follows suit with one of the most succinct guitar solos on the album, a wonder of melody and interesting scale use, verging towards the oriental at the end. The guitar also returns for the coda, resuming the arabesque licks while Eric makes us question the whole fundament of the album by intoning: 'And the jokes are on you, and the jokes are on you'. The song ends in an intense climax that then segues straight into another nursery-like melody, this time played by Allen on the piano accompanied by Albert's hi-hat.

'Astronomy' (A. Bouchard, J. Bouchard, Pearlman)

Then follows the iconic piano intro of what is arguably Blue Öyster Cult's best-loved song, the elegiac 'Astronomy'. A fluid bass underlines the minor key piano progression while a sustained D-note on the synth slowly oscillates in the background. The music sets us up for the lonely seaside scene the lyrics invoke.

> *Come Suzy dear, let's take a walk*
> *Just out there upon the beach*

There is something autumnal and melancholy about this tune that makes it stand out from most other things in the BÖC songbook. Both Albert and Donald apparently had a whack at singing it, but the honour fell to Eric in the end, who displays a very different side to himself as a singer here, conveying the lyrics and melody with a tenderness, albeit with a dark undertone, that is quite unexpected.

A brief word on the melody's key, E minor. This is of course a popular key for guitarist songwriters, as it can ring with pleasant open strings. But it is also a key of note in music history. Classical composers considered the key of E minor to convey both mournfulness and restlessness, and that takes us to the core of the song.

On the surface at least, this is a story of a woman who is soon to be married

('I know you'll soon be married/And you'll want to know where winds come from'), and wants to have some last-minute carnal experiences before she surrenders her freedom. In other words, she may both be mourning the passing of her previous, carefree life, and feel restless for new experiences.

To understand this better we need to take time, with this pivotal song, to dive a bit deeper into the lyrics. Accepted wisdom says that 'Astronomy' was partly inspired by the lesbian experimentation of a girlfriend of Sandy's, Suzy, or Susie. 'Astronomy' once again introduces Suzy, Sandy Pearlman's girlfriend, who at the time was very experimental and sexually aware. This song has its roots in Suzy's lesbian encounter and the reaction to it', according to Bolle Gregmar. (*Morning Final #12*)

The scene, again superficially, seems to tell a story of innocence and experience, a girl who wants to expand her horizon by experiencing more before tying the knot, the 'more' in this case being a lesbian encounter with a girl named Carrie. I mentioned that the song is autumnal in atmosphere. There is a sense of transition, something ending, something new beginning. The time of innocent frolicking, summer, youth, seems to be what is ending. So maybe it is more correct to say the setting is late summer. After all, there is still excitement and sensuality in the air. And what is more sensual than the hot, sultry days of August, the dog days, when people get a little crazy? And why are they called the dog days? Because of the alleged astrological influence of the Dog Star, Sirius. 'Don't forget my dog, fixed and consequent', says Desdinova in the song, referring to Sirius. Yes, it is surely August, the dog days, the month that Imaginos himself was born into the world, according to the myth itself as it unfolds on the album *Imaginos*. And August is also the time of The Reaper, a time for harvest, a time for a season to die before another one begins. Maybe my conclusions are a little heady, but surely Sandy would have wanted it that way.

In his own words,

> *Desdinova walks into the Four Winds Bar (which was a real place – an actual joint on Atlantic Beach). He plays this game with two girls which has to be completed in the six hours from midnight to dawn 'cause he can't stand the light. It's so sort of ... corrosive. There's a parallel with the rose which is similarly over-fulfilled, a symbol of over-ripeness and decadence. The dog is Suzy's familiar and the carrier of starry wisdom from the actual dogstar. Lovecraft had this term 'starry wisdom cult' which was so apt I had to use it. (NME, 1975)*

Heady, in other words.

Having delved into the lyrics, we can now look closer at the music. Joe wrote the verses, which is not hard to hear since they have his unmistakable melancholy imprint on them, something heard in other of his songs like 'Nosferatu' or 'Morning Final' – two other epic and piano-heavy songs. The song starts very serenely, with the verses floating on a bed of reverberated hi-hat and ride cymbals. Then an instrumental melody, harmonised between guitar and organ, enters before the chorus riff takes over. Albert wrote the chorus riff, although 'wrote' is maybe taking it a bit far considering the hook was borrowed more or less wholesale from David Bowie's 'Panic in Detroit'. He gets away with it though, because in the context the riff becomes fully Cult-ized, underpinning the glorious chorus with its anthemic 'hey!'s and Sandy going full mystic with the lyrics.

> *Four winds at the Four Winds Bar*
> *Two doors bought and windows barred*
> *One door to let to take you in*
> *The other one just mirrors it*
> *In hellish glare and inference*
> *The other one's a duplicate*
> *The Queenly flux, eternal light*
> *Or the light that never warms*
> *Yes, the light that never, never warms*
> *Or the light that never*
> *Never warms*

After another verse section the chorus returns, this time augmented by Donald's lead guitar intertwining with Eric's vocals. Then the whole thing breaks down into a quiet section with Albert whipping some effective triplets on the cymbals while Donald engages in some delicate interplay with Joe and Allen, the latter sounding almost like Tony Banks on those early Genesis albums with some impressionistic organ. Then things explode into the final choruses, with the iconic line 'Astronomy – a star' repeated over Donald's ecstatic guitar. Live this song would build to even more epic proportions but here it ends around the 6-and-a-half-minute mark with some cosmic wind effects – it is, after all, the '70s.

Secret Treaties was the definitive Blue Öyster Cult statement up to that point, and to many fans it remains the seminal, defining BÖC album. The production was finally befitting of the music, the songs were their strongest and most concise yet, and as musicians they had grown so much since the first album. Not to mention that this was the album where we finally started to see the real outlines of Sandy's monumental *Imaginos* myth. John Shirley, godfather of cyberpunk and lyricist on the Cult's most recent albums, tells me that *Secret Treaties* was 'the culmination (until *Imaginos*) of the mythos. 'Astronomy' used hints, clues, poetry, to build a mysterious structure in our minds.'

Bolle Gregmar, Cult archivist and all-knower, feels that 'it is lyrically obtuse enough to give a listener many hours of pondering, and is both energy-intensive but at the same time subtle, which is a knack Blue Öyster Cult has which most other bands do not. The lyrics and music are a many-layered universe, where you can peel away layer after layer, exploring each deeper one until you're satisfied that you've reached what the song means to you. And, listening again later might bring you yet another, completely different meaning.' (*MF12*)

Given the strength of the album it is not surprising that it has also left behind quite a legacy. A lot of younger metal fans had their eyes opened to Blue Öyster Cult when Metallica released their *Garage Inc.* album in 1998, featuring a very satisfying cover of 'Astronomy'. In interviews the Metallica guys were only too happy to talk about the influence of Blue Öyster Cult. In an interview with *Rolling Stone*, Metallica drummer Lars Ulrich said of the Cult: 'They were sort of part of that New York intellectual scene that Lou Reed and the Velvet Underground came from. This is a little more thought out and little bit smarter compared to the sort of Neanderthal approach that some other rock bands had at the time. It has a finesse to it.'

Among other notable covers from *Secret Treaties* is hip psych-proggers Espers' cover of 'Flaming Telepaths', which brings a sort of Wicker Man mysticism to the proceedings.

And last but not least, I am sure most BÖC fans were surprised when Harry Potter writer J. K. Rowling under her crime pseudonym Robert Galbraith, published a bestselling book called *Career of Evil*. The book also contained more than fifty snippets of lyrics and titles from Blue Öyster Cult, including a reference to 'The Girl that Love Made Blind', an unreleased song from the *Imaginos* project that only hardcore fans know about. Rowling herself has been tight-lipped about her ideas behind the book but has said, 'It was fun too weaving in the great lyrics of Blue Öyster Cult.'

A quick note on the bonus tracks that appeared on the 2001 remastered version and subsequently on the Columbia box set. While the bonus tracks for the remastered debut had just been some old Soft White Underbelly tracks, and the *Tyranny and Mutation* bonus tracks were contemporaneous live tracks, *Secret Treaties* actually offered up some real unreleased studio tracks. 'Boorman the Chauffeur' is a Steppenwolf-eque rocker with lyrics by Murray Krugman and music by Joe. It does not live up to the high standards of the rest of the album, but it's an interesting and humorous take on the WWII theme of the album, Boorman referring to Hitler's secretary Martin Boorman. The idea of a sinister limo chauffeur was picked up again by Murray for the cover of *On Your Feet or On Your Knees*.

'Mommy' is a bit of bluesy silliness from Eric with words from Meltzer, so over-the-top that it was unsuitable for release. In this day and age, the misogyny of that song would have caused an uproar:

> *I hate my mother, I hate my wife*
> *I'd like to kill em both, it's a fact of life!*
> *I'd like to plan it now, I'm gonna use a knife!*

The most interesting bonus track is Allen's bouncy 'Mes Dames Sarat'. Like so many of Allen's tunes it's got a very good rhythmic foundation and a riff that's like a sped-up Booker T and the MGs riff. The lyrics reference voodoo, and had *Secret Treaties* been released in the CD age, this song surely would have made the cut. It is both musically captivating and lyrically fitting. An interesting thing about the lyrics is the reference to the *Loa*, the spirit creatures of voodoo that are also referred to as Les Invisibles, who we will encounter again in 1988's *Imaginos*.

> *Candy called down the cul-de-sac*
> *And men once dead, come rolling back*
> *To Mes Dames Sarat, men, they kissed her hand*
> *On the sweet, sweet places on the holy plans*
> *They said, 'Coca-Cola voodoo, living mambo, loa, loa, fool*
> *Coca-Cola voodoo, living mambo'*

Chapter 5: Don't report this!
Agents of Fortune (Columbia, 1976)

Personnel:
Eric Bloom: stun guitar, percussion, lead vocals
Donald 'Buck Dharma' Roeser: lead guitar, vocals
Allen Lanier: keyboards, rhythm guitar, vocals
Joe Bouchard: bass, vocals
Albert Bouchard: drums, percussion, acoustic guitar, vocals
Additional musicians:
Patti Smith: vocals on 'The Revenge of Vera Gemini'
Randy Brecker: horns
Michael Brecker: horns
David Lucas: vocals, keyboards, percussion
Produced at The Record Plant, New York 1975-1976 by Murray Krugman, Sandy Pearlman, David Lucas
Release date: May 1976
Highest chart places: 29 (US)
Running time: 36:35

Something happened after *Secret Treaties*. The album sold well, peaking at 53 on the *Billboard* charts. The word on the street was that this was a band in its prime, well worth seeing. The subsequent tour, which covered both the usual areas like the Midwest and the South, also took in California and Canada. The band toured with, among others, T-Rex, Manfred Mann's Earth Band and Kiss. I'll cover the live album that resulted in a separate chapter on live output. Suffice it to say that the live album, *On Your Feet or On Your Knees*, was a surprise hit, rising to 22 on the *Billboard 200*. This opened the door to a new mindset and gave the band new confidence in their abilities. It was this combination of finely-honed skills, confidence and a taste for success that resulted in 1976's *Agents Of Fortune*, the band's definitive breakthrough album.

It was also an album that was partly facilitated by advances in technology. Each member of the band had gotten themselves portable 4-track tape recorders at that point, enabling them to develop and record demos of their songs at home. This meant that there was less reliance on the old 'jam it up at rehearsal' approach to songwriting and more focus on each individual's output. The result was Blue Öyster Cult's most diverse album to that date, and the most fully realised collection of songs they had produced so far in their career.

Eric Bloom explained some of the impact the technology had on the album. 'We were getting more successful, which allowed everybody to go out and get four-track machines. Buck is a very good engineer, and he wrote '(Don't Fear) The Reaper' at home, made a very good demo and came in with it. It sounded very polished right from the start.' (Interview with *Musicradar*)

Bolle Gregmar elucidated on the process:

'Agents Of Fortune was the result of this new step in their creative process, and defined a new method of how an album's material was chosen. For a song to appear on an album, it actually has to fight its way through several stages to finally make it to the final cut. This evolutionary chain could be broken down in three steps: 1) home demo, to be presented first at a band meeting and hopefully chosen to be worked on further, 2) Pre-production demos, which are all basically live versions from band rehearsals (with perhaps some vocals and guitars added on afterwards to present a clearer idea for the producer to work with) and 3) Studio sessions, the selected 'winners' go into the 'real' studio to be properly recorded for inclusion on the released product.' (Morning Final #6)

'This Ain't the Summer of Love' (Albert Bouchard, Murray Krugman, Don Waller)

Even though *Agents Of Fortune* is generally seen as the Cult's first really polished album, and their first foray into radio-tailored songs – which is not untrue – the first impression you get putting on the record is that they have delved even deeper into the then fresh NY punk sound.

The album opens with the anti-hippie anthem 'This Ain't the Summer of Love', which starts characteristically with a staccato guitar augmented by guitar sound effects mimicking bombs falling and exploding, before the song bursts into its punky power chords and Eric contemptuously spitting out the words. With the exception of Allen's organ underneath the aggressive guitars, this is more Ramones than The Doors, and an invigorating update to the BÖC sound. Of course, part of the story here is that the song is strictly not their own. This is reflected in the credits, that include one Don Waller. Don Waller was the lead singer of semi-legendary LA garage rockers Imperial Dogs. They performed 'This Ain't the Summer of Love' as early as 1974, but that version is quite different, both musically and lyrically – apart from the refrain bit with 'this ain't the garden of eden/this ain't the summer of love'.

Apparently, Don Waller had sent the lyrics to Murray Krugman, who had liked the basic idea but changed 90% of the lyrics into what they became on *Agents Of Fortune*. The band also claims that the actual music was borrowed from some Irish activist band, but the song strikes me as mostly a mutation of the Imperial Dogs one. The story is a bit murky. Suffice it to say that it is easy to see how both Murray and Sandy would have been fascinated by the LA proto-punk band who pronounced death to the Summer of Love and performed with swastikas on stage. Both lyrically and musically the song feeds right into Sandy's obsession with the Altamont and the tipping point where rock moved from flowery dreaming to a potentially dark and revolutionary force.

> *Lock all your doors from the outside*
> *The key will dangle by the inside*
> *You may begin to understand*
> *That this is the night we ride*
>
> *This ain't the garden of Eden*
> *There ain't no angels above*
> *And things ain't like they used to be*
> *And this ain't the summer of love*

It is also worth mentioning that this song was covered by certified BÖC fan David Tibet with his industrial/neo-folk outfit Current 93 on their 1988 album *Swastikas for Noddy*, continuing the controversial legacy of this song.

'True Confessions' (Allen Lanier)

The tone changes somewhat with the next song, Allen's 'True Confessions'. It's in many ways a typical Allen song, with a bouncy r'n'b rhythm and a '50s tinge to the chord progressions. But the darkness does not leave us entirely, seeing as this is a tale of 'modern love', with both the forbidden pleasures and emotional complications that entails:

> *True, true confessions*
> *She cried*
> *Stand in the doorway in a jealous rage*
> *Drag myself 'cross her wild terrain*
>
> *We're never sorry*
> *We're never sad*
> *We're modern lovers*
> *What fun we had*

It wouldn't be too far a stretch to guess that the song describes Allen's turbulent relationship with Patti Smith at the time. Allen takes a rare lead vocal here, something the band really should have allowed him to do more often, as he injects just the right amount of seediness and desperation to make the lyrics utterly believable. Another unusual aspect of the song is the sudden appearance of a saxophone solo – a first but not last for the band – performed by session cat Michael Brecker.

It becomes obvious during 'True Confessions' that *Agents Of Fortune* is a quantum leap forward in terms of production values. The onslaught of 'This Ain't the Summer of Love' didn't allow for such subtleties, but in 'Confessions' you can hear a wider and clearer stereo separation, a finely balanced drum mix and a whole new bass tone for Joe – both meaty and with plenty of trebly clarity on top. This was a band aiming for the big league, and the production team of Pearlman/Krugman/Lucas were ably helped in that endeavour by legendary mixer Shelly Yakus, whose impeccable credentials stretch from John Lennon to U2. The band also relocated to the Record Plant, NY for the recording.

Donald told *Mix Magazine* in a 2009 interview, 'Cheap Trick had been there, Aerosmith had been there, Blondie was there. We felt that we needed to access this pool of success and talent so that we could sell some records.'

So clearly the investment in higher fidelity was part of a conscious plan to reach a wider audience.

'(Don't Fear) The Reaper' (Roeser)

Nowhere was this newfound sonic confidence more evident than in the haunting, spectral tones of '(Don't Fear) The Reaper'. Inarguably the Cult's best-known song and a radio staple since its release, 'The Reaper' hit a nerve that few could have anticipated, including its writer, Donald. The song came out of his experiments with his 4-track tape recorder, and his demo was recreated practically note for note on the album.

'In the moment of creation, I had no idea what the world would think of the song. It's been gratifying to see something that has rippled out to the larger culture' (*Mix Magazine*, 2009), Donald has said.

And ripple it did. In 1978 the song appeared in John Carpenter's seminal horror movie *Halloween*, in fact the only music in the movie not composed by Carpenter himself. In the same year Stephen King published his epic novel *The Stand* that quotes the song's lyrics at the beginning of the book. Later usages of the song include a cover version in the post-modern horror comedy *Scream* (1996) and the song is a central plot concern in stoner comedy *The Stoned Age* (1994). It appears in the 2009 Woody Harrelson zombie movie *Zombieland* and most recently has been part of the pre-release strategy for the computer game *Vampyr*, driven by a very contemporary-sounding electronic version of the song. And that's just skimming the surface of the song's appearances. Also, I'm going to spare you more mentions of the 'More cowbell' skit …

So, what exactly makes the song so appealing? There are many elements that add to the haunting nature of the song. It is built around a chiming and beautiful arpeggiated guitar figure reminiscent of the kind Roger McGuinn would use on the old Byrds albums. While McGuinn would achieve that chiming, bell-like quality by playing his 12-string Rickenbacker, Donald achieved a similar effect by layering several guitar sounds. In their article on the recording of the album, *Mix Magazine* delved into the minutia of recording that guitar figure:

> *'To capture the song's signature guitar riff, Yakus recorded four tracks of guitar: a direct feed, one SM57 and one Beyer 160 close-miked on Roeser's*

MusicMan 410 combo amp, and one Neumann U87 as a distant room mic. The guitar tracks were sent through an EMT plate and then recorded on an MCI 24-track. A 15 ips tape delay was recorded right on some of the guitar tracks during the recording.'

The digest version of this is that you had a lot of layers of sound, all with their own frequency characteristics, creating a lot of harmonic motion within an otherwise simple progression.

On top of this came Donald's elegiac melody, delivered in his typically smooth and boyish voice and layered with gorgeous, folk rock-inspired harmonies. The rhythm accompaniment was simple and subdued. Albert says that he mainly followed the rhythmic lead laid down by Donald on the demo, where he was drumming on cardboard boxes.

The gentle, if ghostly, atmosphere of the verses and refrains comes to an end with a crash of cymbals before Donald picks up the guitar again with a foreboding, minor key ostinato (repeated pattern) that keeps repeating while delayed hi-hats sneak in underneath. Then the whole thing explodes with massive chords and a soaring solo played predominantly in the Middle Eastern-sounding Phrygian mode. The solo section is brilliant in that it both brings out all the latent darkness of the song, really illustrating the arrival of 'The Reaper' while it also retains a strong harmonic relationship with the rest of the song. It is an absolute musical highlight in the entire BÖC oeuvre and astonishingly, Donald's solo was captured in one take. The solo climaxes with tense snare rolls and finally an 'infinitely' sustained note from Donald that fades into a return to the verses.

Love of two is one
Here but now they're gone
Came the last night of sadness
And it was clear that she couldn't go on
And the door was open and the wind appeared
The candles blew and then disappeared
The curtains flew and then he appeared

Saying don't be afraid
Come on, baby
And she had no fear
And she ran to him

Donald's lyrics for this song are almost painfully poetic and prove that the Cultsters could stand very well on their own feet, lyrically speaking. A tale of love that transcends the boundaries of mortality, it was inspired by Donald's own early musings on issues of life and death.

'I was thinking about mortality. The whole idea of 'The Reaper' was that if there was another sphere of existence, maybe lovers could bridge that gap if their love was strong enough.' (Interview, *New York Times*, 2016)

Maybe one shouldn't try too hard to analyse why a certain song just seems to move almost everyone who hears it. But a painstaking, layered approach to production, a thoughtful arrangement, songwriting that straddles the sublime and the sinister and lyrics that deal with the two most timeless themes in literary history – love and death – can't really go wrong. Shelly Yakus allegedly exclaimed after the recording: 'Guys, this is it! The legendary once-in-a-lifetime groove!'

'E.T.I. (Extra Terrestrial Intelligence)' (Roeser, Pearlman)

The casual FM rock listener would be forgiven for thinking that *Agents Of Fortune* wouldn't have much to offer beyond 'The Reaper'. But as it happens, the song is followed by yet another highlight. 'E.T.I. (Extra Terrestrial Intelligence)' offers a lot, both musically and lyrically. The music is Donald's, and the song opens with a signature guitar riff that wouldn't have been out of place on the first two albums. The difference being that here it is augmented by a hi-tech gizmo, the talk box. Made famous by Pete Frampton, Roger Troutman and Richie Sambora, the history of this contraption actually goes back to the late '30s, when steel guitarist Alvino Rey modified some army tech to create a microphone that could modulate the frequency content of the guitar signal by grafting the frequency profile of the human voice on top. In simpler terms, you could make the guitar 'talk' and 'sing'. By 1976 it was still not the best-known effect, although it soon would be, since it was also the year of Frampton Comes Alive. But it certainly added an extra layer of strangeness to the otherwise otherworldly 'E.T.I.'

As the drums enter, we are treated to liberal doses of reverb reminiscent of that soft-focus sound on the first album – the kick drum positively blossoms with dense reverb. But Shelly Yakus knew when to pour it on and when to hold it back, and as the whole band enters, he pulls out the reverb on the kick drum so that it cuts through the dense sound, while he retains it on the snare, letting it float on top of the mix. The effect is that of the tightening of a bolt. In the beginning things feel a bit untethered, but then everything comes together in sharp focus as the full band takes the riff, and the vocals enter. Lyrics courtesy of Sandy Pearlman, in fact his only lyrical contribution on the album.

I'm in fairy rings and tower beds
'Don't report this' three men said
Books by blameless and by the dead
King in yellow, the Queen in red

All praise
He's found the awful truth

Balthazar
He's found the saucer news

On an album that stands out as light on conceptuality but strong on individual song performances, this is the only nod to the Pearlman universe, and a good one at that. Pearlman, being the gothic horror aficionado he was, manages to reference Robert W. Chambers, one of Lovecraft's favourite writers, in a song that is otherwise about flying saucers and 'men in black'. *The King in Yellow* is Chambers' most famous book, and one in which he pretty much invented the kind of self-contained parallel universe ploy that Lovecraft would later use in his Cthulhu mythos, and Pearlman after him with *Imaginos*. Pearlman was aware of the historical lineage of what he was doing, and cleverly pulls together the archaic and the modern in his juxtaposition of 'the king in yellow, the queen in red' and the 'men in black'.

The sci-fi quotient is further increased by Allen's addition of a tremulous synthesiser line in the refrain, imitating that typical '50s B-movie sound effect, the theremin. Guitar-wise, this song is a real showcase for Donald. His solo spots show a new sense of economy and conciseness, less Jerry Garcia and more hooks. Especially the ending solo is a wonder of melodic simplicity and grace. Live, 'E.T.I.' would unfold into a prog rock extravaganza, the song shifting gears into breakneck speeds while Donald would shower the audiences with guitar pyrotechnics. The version on 1978's *Some Enchanted Evening* is a good example.

'The Revenge of Vera Gemini' (A. Bouchard, Patti Smith)

Not wanting to lose momentum, the band closes out side A with yet another classic and deep cut, 'The Revenge of Vera Gemini'. Penned and sung by Albert, it has lyrics by Patti Smith, and more significantly, features the first guest vocal performance on a Cult album by none other than Patti herself. Before the music starts, Patti sets the mood with this incantation:

You're boned like a saint
With the consciousness of a snake

The music enters, beautifully mixed with a twangy guitar in the right channel and Joe on a syncopated but simple bass guitar line with a bass sound to die for and spacious drums. The vocals are treated to a rich and plentiful delay/reverb effect, but because everything is so meticulously balanced and placed, both left/right and back/front, the overall sense is of an uncluttered and spacious arrangement. Albert holds the lead vocal for the duration of the song, but Patti interjects little comments along the way. The effect is of a romantic tug and war, but as so often with the Cult, with sombre and sultry undertones. Allen enhances the atmosphere with subtle piano and what sounds like layered organ and string synth. Much has been made of the lyrics. One interpretation asserts that the '24th of May' referred to in the song references both Albert and Bob Dylan's birthday, and that this particular lyric was given to Albert as a birthday gift and tells the story of an encounter between Patti and Bob Dylan.

Patti, who had released her album *Horses* the year before, also plays a bit of a joke on herself when she makes Albert sing:

> *Oh, no more horses, horses*
> *We're going to swim like a fish*
> *Into the hole in which you planned to ditch me*
> *My lovely, Vera Marie!*

But whatever one might make of the lyrics, this is a strong end to side A, reminiscent of other moody slow burners from earlier albums, like 'Subhuman' and 'Workshop of the Telescopes'.

'Sinful Love' (A. Bouchard, Helen Wheels)

Side B of *Agents of Fortune* kicks off with a bit of an odd one-two punch, the first a tight, taut little rock'n'roll number called 'Sinful Love' that Albert wrote to lyrics by the enigmatic Helen Robbins, later known as Helen Wheels.

To understand the first two songs on side B we first need to know a little about Helen Wheels, who wrote the lyrics for both of them. She was a student at Stony Brook at the same time as Sandy, and according to Richard Meltzer she quickly transformed from a quiet, shy girl to a mescaline-dealing amazon who used to hang around the band and became friendly with Albert. Whether or not we choose to believe the legends, it is a fact that Helen became something of a figure in the burgeoning East Coast punk scene, and it was The Dictators' 'Handsome' Dick Manitoba who gave her the moniker Helen Wheels (otherwise known as a Wings song about Paul and Linda's car). By all accounts she lived an unusual life, doing body-building, picking fights with fans at concerts with her Helen Wheels Band, relating tales of her own alien abductions and eventually finding some peace in new age magic before her untimely death in 2000.

'Sinful Love' was her first contribution to the band, and it seems to be a story of someone who has grown frightfully tired and annoyed by their lover and fantasises about ending things in violent ways while still harbouring some attraction to the fella, or girl depending on your perspective.

> *You're over my shoulder, I think I'm possessed*
> *Your constant undertone is making me toothless*
> *Time's come to trim you gonna get out my knife*
> *Gonna cut you out baby, out of my life*

> *Daredevil, She-devil, Printer's devil, Evil*
> *I love you like sin, but I won't be your pigeon*
> *Daredevil, She-devil, Printer's devil, Evil*
> *I love you like sin, but I won't be your pigeon*

Musically the song is an interesting mixture of '50s pastiche (the pounding Jerry Lee Lewis piano and the high-pitched harmony vocals) and muscular hard rock, a concept the band would revisit on *Mirrors*, and the song is led along by a strong lead vocal from Albert. It is not the most profound track on the album, but it starts side B off with energy and zest.

'Tattoo Vampire' (A. Bouchard, Wheels)

There is hardly a pause before the most striking song opening on the album hits us. The repeated, hard strumming on a muted guitar chord along with a pounding kick drum sounds like a locomotive gaining momentum before it bursts into the heavy-rocking riff of 'Tattoo Vampire'. The textures of the guitars are dense and shiny, the result of meticulously layered recordings, and Albert rides his drums like a man possessed, sounding at his most Bonhamesque. This is probably the heaviest and most intense song on the album, and fittingly Eric is behind the microphone again. He is sounding rather evil on these lyrics that allegedly deal with an unfortunate encounter between a psychopathic boyfriend, a drunk and passed-out girlfriend and a nervous tattooist. According to Helen herself, a Warhol hang-around held Helen's tattoo artist friend at knife-point to get him to tattoo his name on his unconscious girlfriend's buttocks. Such is the high life in those artist circles. The song works better without knowing all the details, especially since it is dressed up in vampire trappings and fits in well with other BÖC vampire tales like 'Nosferatu' and 'I Love the Night'.

> *I went down last night with a tattoo madame*
> *To a nude dagger fantasy domain*
> *Wrapped in hell, I lost my breath…Whoa!*
> *Chest to stimulating Chinese breast*
>
> *Grisly smiles that don't flake off*
> *Carny colored demons leering*
> *Vampire photo suckin' the skin*
> *Vampire, Tattoo Vampire*

The song has a couple of interesting similarities with 'The Reaper': The refrain features some arpeggiated guitar chords with an open string chiming along with the fretted notes, just like in 'The Reaper', and there is a tense middle solo section that features a similar underlying ostinato to the one in 'The Reaper', but this time played by the bass. A cool production trick in the refrain is a synth-like vibrato effect on the voice that is either the result of the vocal being run through a synth or a deft superimposition of synth and voice.

'Morning Final' (J. Bouchard)
With another breathless transition we are over in a very different sonic world, with some almost serene piano chords and a melancholy, stately guitar melody played on top. It's not hard to spot the epic mind of Joe at work here. The cinematic scope of the intro of 'Morning Final' narrows down to a solid groove held by both guitar, piano and organ and a slightly funky beat from Albert. There is a lot of colour and texture on offer here, in a song that revisits the seedy subways and dangerous streets of New York that Joe likes to write about.

Joe: 'Well, I was actually staying in the city at Patti Smith's apartment with Allen Lanier, our keyboard player. They were living together at the time. We were just sort of crashing at different places. And there was this murder that happened in the subway. And the subway stop was like, maybe, 100 feet from the door where I was staying. So that was the idea. I read about it in the newspaper. And I said, 'oh I got to write a song about this.'' (Interview with *thecollegecrowddigsme.com*)

> *He cast a grim shadow*
> *Through the busy street*
> *Said he was a junkie*
> *And he punctuated his walk with a gun*
>
> *Motiveless murder*
> *The papers screamed*
> *The cops all said*
> *The crowd was iced by the sight*

Joe relates the tale with great conviction and with his trademark vulnerability – it's always a pleasure when Joe takes the lead vocal. The song is the second longest on the album, after 'The Reaper', and takes time for a proggy excursion into double time after a restrained and thematic solo from Donald. The busy beat and an urgent progression illustrate the words as Joe intones: 'Down the subway stairs, after him they leapt' as the police chase the killer. Joe was always a strong storyteller and this song is no exception.

As an aside it's worth noting that the New York summer of '76 into which *Agents Of Fortune* was released, was haunted by the spectre of a very real killer: the Son of Sam, real name David Berkowitz. The chilling themes of this album, and especially 'The Reaper' and 'Morning Final', must have had a special resonance for New Yorkers that summer as they were held in the grip of the Son of Sam's terror.

The song ends as cinematically as it began, with the screeching of train brakes (a clever echo of the locomotive start of 'Tattoo Vampire') and Eric imitating a paper boy shouting, 'Paper! Police say no motive for murder in subway! Paper! Read all about it! Paper, Mister?'

'Tenderloin' (Lanier)

Out of the subway din crawls a twisting, energetic little riff that belongs to 'Tenderloin' – in this writer's opinion Allen's finest contribution to the band. Crisp guitar chords are panned to each side of a rubbery, motownesque bass line while a sinuous moog-line modulates in the background. There is both funk and a bit of jazziness to be traced here, but interestingly the lead vocal is given to Eric, which ensures the rock credentials in this simmering, heat-struck story of love and cocaine gone wrong.

> *I come to you in a blue, blue room*
> *By some abuse and some heart*
> *You raise the blinds say*
> *Let's have light on life*
> *Let's watch it fall apart*
> *Let's watch it fall apart*
>
> *Nighttime flowers*
> *Evening roses*
> *Bless this garden that never closes*
> *Treat her gently*
> *Treat her kind*
> *Tenderloin will last all night*

Again it's reasonable to assume that Allen is writing about experiences with Patti Smith, but the lyrics are so poetic and cryptic that they seem open to multiple interpretations, as so many BÖC lyrics.

The refrain keeps much of the verse groove, especially the semi-walking bass, but changes up the chord progression and adds some echoing keyboard arpeggios, showcasing Allen's tasteful but economic use of his ivories on this album. After another vocal section there is a break with some darker, descending chords played by guitar and clavinet, before an absolutely gorgeous but brief moog solo elaborates the verse melody. This is followed by some crisp start/stop chording and a sensual, surf-like guitar line that drifts across the stereo image, before a recap of the vocal section that is given new urgency by quicker-paced passing chords played by Donald. After the last refrain we are treated to an almost raga-like guitar section with propulsive, elegant drums from Albert and more oriental modes from Donald, yet the transition from the refrain feels natural and unforced. Then there is yet another change as the verse accompaniment returns but this time harmonised by descending guitar lines and eventually an ornate, multi-tracked guitar melody employing hammer-on/pull-off techniques before a quick, final crescendo.

I describe the progression of this song in detail because I consider it a small miracle both in terms of songwriting and arrangement. In just three and a half minutes Allen manages to include so much musical excitement in the song while still retaining a flow and groove that feels uninterrupted. This is a testament to unusual compositional capabilities that were unfortunately underused in the band. Whether this was a question of band politics or because Allen's struggles with his lifestyle made him less prolific, remains an open question, but with 'Tenderloin' he left an indelible mark on the BÖC corpus.

'Debbie Denise' (A. Bouchard, Patti Smith)

Had the album ended here, it would have been a perfect A+ of an album. But unfortunately, as many Cult fans agree, there is one more track, 'Debbie Denise'. This Albert/Patti Smith tune is not exactly bad, but it simply does not live up to the incredibly high standards of the rest of the album and seems like a needless addition that mood-wise is incompatible with the rest of the material. With a synth bass, symphonic-sounding string synth and shimmering 12-string acoustic guitar it is sonically appealing, but it strictly sounds more like a ballad out of a Styx album (not that there is anything wrong with that!) than a Blue Öyster Cult song. There is something too light-hearted and silly about the high-pitched, cheerful harmonies in the chorus, and something insubstantial about the sound of it. On a weaker album it may have stood its ground, but on *Agents Of Fortune* it falls short.

Apart from that one misstep, *Agents Of Fortune* has to be considered an extremely successful record – obviously commercially, but especially musically. It doesn't have the unity of sound or the conceptual coherence of Secret Treaties, but instead it is a collection of songs that are so strong, so well-produced and arranged, and displaying such a stylistic diversity that it is hard to think of any other hard rock band that matched the Cult's maturity in the mid-'70s.

There is only one Pearlman lyric here, and no mention of Desdinova or Imaginos, but somehow the band managed to sound just as mysterious and cryptic as on previous albums, even showing that their own lyrics could be just as artful as those of a Smith or a Meltzer. And with less of the conceptual weight to pull, the band displayed a lighter, more colourful touch both musically and lyrically.

Response to the album matched its inherent qualities. Ken Tucker raved in his *Rolling Stone* review: '*Agents Of Fortune*' is a startlingly excellent album – startling because one does not expect Blue Öyster Cult to sound like this: loud but calm, manic but confident, melodic but rocking. Every song on the first side is commercially accessible without compromising the band's malevolent stance.' He even singled out Donald's guitar on 'Tenderloin': 'Buck Dharma's agile guitar lines on 'Tenderloin' are far more effective than his heretofore standard thudding meanness.'

Hipster rag *Crawdaddy* called the album 'intensely melodic, laced with icy Frisco guitar leads ... Scary is still beautiful but 'Agents' manages to toss some hefty lyrical ballast into the raging metal torrent that has long been BÖC's stock in trade.'

And the album made it to many 'best of 1976' lists. But most importantly, of course, was the fact that Blue Öyster Cult had their first bona fide hit single. '(Don't Fear) The Reaper' the single, backed with 'Tattoo Vampire', spent an impressive twenty weeks in the Billboard Hot 100, peaking at twelve and holding that position for two entire weeks. Blue Öyster Cult finally had what every hard rock band wished they could have – a crossover single that appealed to rockers and pop fans alike and that sounded like it was simply made for FM radio. To this day the song is in regular rotation on classic rock stations across the world. The single pulled the album along with it too: Agents spent 35 weeks in the album charts, climbing as high as #32 in November. By 1978 the album would be certified platinum – over 1,000,000 records sold. The freaks from Long Island had made it.

Chapter 6: The station of night
Spectres (Columbia 1977)
Personnel:
Eric Bloom: guitar, vocals
Donald "Buck Dharma" Roeser: lead and rhythm guitars, vocals
Allen Lanier: keyboards, guitar, vocals
Joe Bouchard: bass guitar, guitar, vocals
Albert Bouchard: drums, harmonica, vocals
Additional musicians:
Newark Boys Chorus: vocals on 'Golden Age of Leather'
Produced at The Record Plant, New York, July-September 1977 by Murray Krugman, Sandy Pearlman, David Lucas, Blue Öyster Cult
UK release date: November 1977
Highest chart places: 43 (US), 60 (UK)
Running time: 40:29

Aurora. Spellbinder. Night Vision. Chamber of Dreams. Night Delivery. Hot Nights. Night of the Fantastic.
There was little doubt about the atmosphere the Cult wanted to convey with *Spectres*. The above titles are from a notebook where they recorded viable suggestions for a title for what became *Spectres*. It was all about the mysteries of night, or as Donald put it, the soul on the other side of the earth.

Spectres is a strange album. The band felt a lot of pressure after the success of *Agents* and were not shy to admit that they wanted to replicate the success.

'We are looking for a hit', explained Murray Krugman in *Modern Recording* back in 1977. 'The album comes across as very diverse, which most people think is an asset. But when you have five people writing material, each in a totally different universe ...' The almost apologetic tone was reflected in other interviews as well. 'I admit on *Spectres* we tried to be as commercial as we could', said Allen in a 1978 interview. Sandy was no less candid about it, and told *NME*, '*Spectres* is a deliberate attempt to make an album that would sell three million units and beat Fleetwood Mac'. And Albert admitted to the 'Unbelievable pressure. And really the thing was, once we had a taste of having a hit, that became the criteria of what would make it onto this record. We'd gone from trying to be very different than everybody else, and if it sounded too commercial we wouldn't do it on the first three records. Then we had success. We had money. All of a sudden we were filling huge halls and headlining. We wanted to continue that. I would say that if *Spectres* had a weakness, it would be that we started feeling materialistic about the whole thing.' (Interview with the *Austin Chronicle*)

I see a bit of an interesting and complicated juxtaposition here. On the one hand the band had a strong artistic vision towards making a record about nocturnal mysteries, the nightside of the human soul. Very Blue Öyster Cult, and interestingly without much input from Sandy. On the other hand, the band were desperate for another hit, and were excited about moving in a more mainstream, commercial direction. There were many good reasons for this. The members of the band were getting older, some had become parents, so a more stable lifestyle and economy were desirable. Another reason was more artistic: They had grown tired of the heavy metal pigeonholing and saw that they could successfully diversify their style after the success of *Agents*.

Another, much more pragmatic consideration was that they needed to cover the cost of the enormously expensive laser rigs they brought with them on tour at that point. 'We can't afford to be a strictly cult group', Donald mused in the same *NME* interview.

The successful pursuit of both commercial success and of that 'night vision' was further complicated by the fact that touring broke up the recording. The band wrote and worked on one batch of songs, then went on tour before they came back and wrote and recorded another batch. Additionally, the total studio time was considerably less than for *Agents*.

All this led to an album of high ambitions, but it was also the first time cracks began to show in the Cult's hitherto indestructible artistic foundation. The album does have a strong atmosphere, further enhanced by the red-hot glowing cover showing the band in some arcane, old library shot through with laser beams. One imagines the bookshelves must be full of books like the *Necronomicon*. Song titles like 'Death Valley Nights' and 'I Love the Night' are also evocative. Knowing that the album was recorded between July and September of 1977 in New York, we get an additional insight into the atmosphere of the album: That was the summer of a historically intense heatwave – and also, still, a time when killer David Berkowitz stalked the streets (he was finally apprehended on August 10 that summer). New Yorkers refer to it as the 'Summer of Sam', a summer of hot, nervous nights.

On the album, especially songs like 'I Love the Night', 'Fireworks', 'Death Valley Nights' and 'Nosferatu' live up to that sultry, sweaty, intense atmosphere. But unfortunately, the album contains both hits and misses. It is clear that the commercial pressures fogged the band's judgment and ability to pick the very best material for the album. Some of the strongest music written in the period was Albert's *Imaginos* songs, but these were shelved as the band did not want another conceptual album at this point. Instead they wanted to diversify and flex their pop muscles. In fact, the album's title gives an indication of where things were headed – *Spectres* is also a sly reference to '60s hit producer Phil Spector and his wall of sound. We will come back to that.

'Godzilla' (Roeser)

The album's monster opening, so to speak, is taken care of by 'Godzilla'. This Donald-penned riff-o-rama has remained a concert staple to this day, and although it was not the hit the label had hoped for, it ensured steady radio play and enduring visibility for the band, post-*Agents*. The song opens characteristically with a simple, heavy riff enhanced by a prominent delay effect and backed by just a kick drum. Then the hi-hats enter, along with a repeating bent-note guitar motif before the vocals come in. Unusually, Donald and Eric share vocals here, at times singing together in unison and at other times harmonising each other. Underneath it all Albert holds one of his grooviest drum beats ever, filled with bouncy syncopations and busy ghost notes. The chorus is basically a blues progression but made special by Donald's pop-tastic vocal hook. Godzilla is in many ways another early example of pop metal, heavy and catchy all at once. The song, as the title implies, relates the story of Godzilla, the famous Japanese monster who was a child of Hiroshima and Nagasaki, a distillation of Japanese nuclear anxiety. It is also a cautionary and moral tale:

> *History shows again and again*
> *How nature points up the folly of man*
> *Godzilla!*

Halfway through the song the band mostly drops out and Joe gets a brief and funky bass solo before the drums join and the rhythm section really steams up. Eric intones 'God-zilla, god-zilla', helped by some special tape effects, and in the background we can hear a Japanese newscaster issuing the following warning (in Japanese):

'We give you special news. We give you special news.
Godzilla is turning towards the Ginza district.
As soon as possible take shelter, please.
As soon as possible take shelter, please.'

A fun, exciting tune that sets the album off on a high note.

'Golden Age of Leather' (Roeser, Bruce Abbott)

The light atmosphere of *Godzilla* seems to continue when the next thing we hear is a drinking song! 'Raise your can of beer on high, and seal your fate forever'. But things quickly take a more serious turn as the actual music of 'Golden Age of Leather' enters. Musically the song is a sort of light take on prog rock, with several sections melded together, but unlike earlier prog excursions that were usually the domain of Joe, this is a Donald tune, so it also has that feather-light pop touch. At times the elegant and structured feel of the music seems at odds with the lyrics. Donald's old college friend Bruce Abbott wrote them, clearly with Sandy's Altamont/biker mythos in mind. It is a futuristic, almost apocalyptic vision of the last days of the Hells Angels. They are a dying breed, and meet at a roadhouse for a last drink, and then a last battle. They split up into bands, marked by rags they carry in one of two colours – red and black, of course. And then they fight unto death. Abbott had written the lyrics during the oil crisis and he and others with him had thought that both Harleys and biker culture in general were going the way of the dodo, thus the subject matter. The lyrics are quite remarkable. While they retain the mythic edge of

Sandy's lyrics, they have a different clarity and a deeply poetic quality.

> *And there was worn no cloth but leather*
> *Made supple by years of stinging cinders*
> *And here were seen the scars of age*
> *For age had been the common call for one last night together*
>
> *Dawn colored the sky: The ritual ceased*
> *Some had died: And they were buried with their bikes*
> *Each grabbed a rag: From a man with a sack*
> *Torn strips of colour: The red and the black*

The song is very ambitious, boy choirs and all, and the 'Dawn colored the sky' section approaches the actual drama of the words, but all in all 'Golden Age of Leather' is a rare occasion in the Cult corpus where the music falls somewhat short of the lyrics. The production doesn't help. While it is pristine and professional, it lacks in meat and grit, and the arrangement, while ambitious, also feels under-worked – a probable result of the time-restraints on the production.

'Death Valley Nights' (A. Bouchard, Richard Meltzer)
As I've touched upon, the main bulk of Albert's song production at this point was the *Imaginos* song cycle that he was working on with Sandy. Since that avenue was considered too non-commercial for *Spectres*, he had to turn in something simpler instead. By his own admission, Albert was never happy with what he turned in for *Spectres*, which maybe says more about his inner critic than the actual material. His first contribution on *Spectres* was 'Death Valley Nights', a moody, piano-led ballad with lyrics by Richard Meltzer. It's a well-written tune with a bit of a country rock feel that wouldn't have been out of place on a '70s Eagles record. Not exactly what you'd expect on a BÖC record, but then neither are a lot of the songs on *Spectres*. The chorus is classic Cult with some nice guitar riffing and luscious, layered harmonies. The arrangement is fairly straight-forward and I can imagine that had *Spectres* been given the luxurious time-frame of *Agents*, this song would have been more fleshed out. As it is, the simplicity brings our focus to the words, and they are some of Meltzer's finest.

> *Bleached by the sun*
> *And scorched by the moon*
> *If I make it 'til tomorrow noon I'm leaving*
>
> *'Tween the horror of space*
> *And the terror of time*
> *My heart in crystal down the line I'm screaming*

There's no clear story-line, and Meltzer himself has called the lyrics a 'tone-poem', partly inspired by a trip with a Manson-obsessed girlfriend to Death Valley.

'Searchin' For Celine' (Lanier)
A piano is central as the next song enters as well, but it's a bit of a false start because after that intro we are treated to a trademark Allen funk groove. 'Searchin' For Celine' is Allen's only contribution on the album. Typically for him, with his love for European decadent poetry and culture, the song is a tribute to controversial French writer Louis-Ferdinand Céline, early modernist and infamous anti-Semite. However, when it came to recording the song it was decided that Eric should take over the lead vocal, and Eric changed the 'he' to a 'she', turning it into a love song instead. It is one of the less successful moves on the record, as Eric's delivery is at odds with the sprightly feel of the song. I believe this could have been a stronger number if Allen himself had sung it and kept the Céline connection clear. As it stands, though, it is not a bad song. The vocal arrangements are quite gorgeous and dare we say Spectoresque, and there is a bridge where Eric sings ...

> *Love is like a gun*
> *And in the hands of someone*
> *Like you I think it'd kill*
> *But oh, what a thrill*
> *Oh, what a thrill*

... that is hands down sublime, complete with a Supertramp-like electric piano pounding out eighths. The song ends with a fade-out two-chord vamp with Donald soloing, but unfortunately the solo is somewhat drowned out by excessive reverb.

'Fireworks' (A. Bouchard)
Side A ends like it started, with a musical highlight. Albert's ballad 'Fireworks' is a lush piece of electrified folk-rock, shimmering with layers of clean, electric guitar arpeggios. In some ways this could have been written by Donald, but Albert's lead vocal gives it away, being much more intimate and vulnerable than Donald's confident and studio-ready vocals. The song is simply but beautifully arranged, with harmony-laced guitar fills that could've come out of an early Thin Lizzy album. The lyrics are very open to interpretation but given the title, the consummation of love is definitely a central theme.

> *She went down to her house by the water*
> *To hide herself from his grasp*
> *He went down to the water to find her*
> *To consummate their love at last*

> *Then the lightning flashing (lightning, flashing, crashing)*
> *Fireworks shooting off in her head (in her head)*
> *The earth was shaking (earth, shaking, quaking)*
> *Fireworks pouring down on her head (on her head)*
> *Only sound she heard was (sound, lovely word)*
> *Fireworks like a charm (anointed)*
> *Blazing red*

This is one of the tracks that reflects the intended mood of the record successfully – there is both dark romance and a chill in the words and in the music.

'R. U. Ready 2 Rock' (A. Bouchard, Sandy Pearlman)

'R. U. Ready 2 Rock' may sound like a Prince song and seems indicative of pure rock goofiness. And while the first track on side B is definitely an entertaining rocker, there is a bit more to it than that. While Albert wrote the music, this is the sole Sandy lyric on the album. There are scant references to Invisibles and *Secret Treaties*, but again this is a call to arms to the rock revolution, the revolution by night.

> *Come on, come on to the cities of night*
> *Come on, come on everybody's praying*
> *Come on, come on for the wonder of light*
> *Come on, come on there's a new day breaking*

The music is a breath of fresh air after all the sultry, nocturnal ruminations on much of side A. The main riffs are memorable and take the listener back to the heavier days of *Tyranny* or *Secret Treaties*, and the song is supported by a drum groove that's built like a tank, rock steady and unrelenting. Like 'Golden Age' the song also moves through several sections, but at greater pace and with more gusto. The whole band seems to come alive after the relative somnambulence of much of the album so far. Eric delivers a classic, intense vocal performance and Donald rips some signature licks that have so far been absent on the album apart from on 'Godzilla'. Production-wise this song is also a winner, with thick, visceral guitar sounds and upfront vocals.

'Celestial the Queen' (J. Bouchard, Helen Wheels)

After this vitamin shot arrives a personal favourite moment on the album, Joe's gorgeous 'Celestial the Queen'. It's an interesting tune in that it picks up a few stylistic cues from a style that was prevalent around the band at the time, but one they had not hitherto dabbled in. Pomp rock was a big genre in the mid-'70s Midwest, which was also the heartland of BÖC's audience. Bands like Styx and Angel made it big with a mixture of melodic hard rock and synthesiser fanfares borrowed from prog rock. And that is exactly what Joe very successfully does in 'Celestial the Queen'. The song begins with dramatic piano and a soaring mini-moog lead from Allen that brings Rick Wakeman to mind, before Joe enters with a yearning, urgent vocal melody. The whole song is given luxurious reverb treatment in a way that again reminds one of Spector's wall of sound. In particular the drums give an enormous and deep sound, with low-tuned snare and toms and a dark reverb, a sound that Journey would replicate with great commercial success with producer Mike Stone in the 1980s. The song ends with a glorious moog solo from Allen that is pure prog rock. It makes you wish Allen would have taken the solo spotlight a lot more often on the synth, as he admittedly did live in the late '70s and early '80s. The lyrics are one of two on the album written by Helen Wheels, whose acquaintance we made on the *Agents* album. It appears to be another vampire-centric lyric with a strong female character, as in many of her songs.

She came from the dark, she came from a dream
All leather and chain the rising Queen
Born into the night, born into the spotlight
She spread her wings and then she was gone

Joe takes the lead vocal here and sounds confident and in the pocket. Although this is not the best-known Cult track and was rarely performed live, it is still one of the highlights of the album.

'Goin' Through the Motions' (Bloom, Ian Hunter)
Next up is Eric's major contribution to the album, the catchy 'Goin' Through the Motions'. Co-written with Eric's friend, Mott the Hoople's Ian Hunter, this song takes the Phil Spector connection to its ultimate conclusion, as the song starts with that classic 'Leader of the Pack' drum groove. The entire song has a strong '60s pop feel and is perhaps the most untypical BÖC song on the album, but it is so well done, so perfectly arranged and played that it is impossible not to be charmed and taken in by it, even if it hardly lives up the album's generally cryptic aura. The musicianship shows great maturity, as each player reins his ego in and simply plays to serve the song in the best possible manner. Eric is also in great form here, showing his most soulful side as a singer.

The bridge section is particularly noteworthy, both for its reference to 'Stairway to the Stars' ('sign it 'Love to you'') and for the heavenly pop progression and harmonies.

To thee I dedicate this photograph
I'll even sign it 'love to you' again
And when it's faded and forgotten in some book
You'll sometimes look

The lyrics may be a commentary on the difficulty of maintaining meaningful and lasting relationships for musicians on the road, something both Eric and Ian would have known about.

The chorus is characterized by Allen's Farfisa-sounding string synth and shamelessly '60s handclaps! Murray Krugman probably summed the song up best when he told *Modern Recording* the song is 'sort of rock and roll pop'.

'I Love the Night' (Roeser)

Side B ends very strongly with the two most atmospheric and moody pieces on the album. First up is Donald's immortal vampire tale 'I Love the Night'. Hailed by most Cult fans as one of the band's greatest ballads, this is also one of the most singularly haunting and beautiful pieces in BÖC's catalogue. The textures of the song are shimmering and ephemeral with clean, chorused electric guitars, drums drenched in reverb, a deep bass occasionally augmented by a synthesiser bass and Donald's voice sounding even more yearning and melancholy than on 'The Reaper'. Of special note are also the wordless vocal harmonies, a precursor of the lush pillows of harmony that supported 'Burnin' For You' a few years later.

There are multiple layers of guitar here, each playing different roles and occupying different spaces both on the soundstage and in the frequency spectrum. The result is a complex, but open sound, further underlined by Donald's arpeggiated guitar progressions, again as in 'The Reaper' depending on open, ringing chords and steering clear of an overtly major/minor tonality, resulting in a sort of questioning, ambivalent feel. Musicologist Brett Clement, in his paper *Modal Tonicization in Rock*, uses 'I Love the Night' as an example of a song with more than one tonal centre, creating an ambivalence that he says is reflected in the lyrics: 'Regarding the narrative of the song, the E-Aeolian verses describe a process of searching, whereby a protagonist walking alone eventually finds comfort in the dark. The attainment of this goal is celebrated in the chorus with the move into 'bright' Lydian tonality. Here, Lydian takes on otherworldly associations, representing a breaking free from the confines of earthly sorrow.'

> *No mortal was meant to know such wonder*
> *One look in the mirror told me so*
> *Come darkness I'll see her again*
> *Yes, I'm gonna go*
> *'Cause now I know*
>
> *I love the night*
> *The day is OK and the sun can be fun but I live*
> *To see those rays slip away*

'I Love the Night' stands as one of Donald's most sensitive and thoughtful contributions to the band and is a song that wholly encapsulates the nocturnal ambience of *Spectres*.

'Nosferatu' (J. Bouchard, Wheels)

If the vampire wave the Cultsters were riding on *Agents* and *Spectres* wasn't clear for everyone by now, Joe certainly drove the point home with his epic song about the original movie vampire, 'Nosferatu'. Moving the scene from his usual streets and subway stations of New York to the Europe of yore, Joe paints a perfect gothic picture with this sweeping, symphonic rock piece.

> *It came together pretty fast actually. I had a studio in my garage with this old white grand piano. And it was pretty much one of those things where I just sat down and improvised. The reason the song happened at all was because we were supposed to do a tour of Canada and it got cancelled. So when I came home for a couple of extra days, I got this lyric from my collaborator, Helen Wheels. She wrote the lyrics and it's pretty much just like she gave it to me. I wrote the music and it worked out really good. It's definitely a fan favourite. (thecollegecrowddigsme.com)*

Lead by a deep mid-tempo groove and a 'Sturm & Drang' Wagnerian piano figure that rises and falls, the song seems a perfect accompaniment to the old black and white movie by Murnau. As Joe's slightly desperate-sounding vocals enter we are also treated to the ghostly tones of the Chamberlin. A precursor of the Mellotron, famous for its use on classic albums by The Moody Blues, King Crimson and Yes, the Chamberlin was the original tape sampler. Each key activated a spool of tape playing back a few seconds of your chosen instrument in the corresponding pitch. The Chamberlin was particularly famous for its string sounds, which were both full but also a little brittle and seasick, creating a rich and slightly creepy sound. The Chamberlin also had the advantage of stereo recorded sounds, as opposed to the mono Mellotron. It is exactly the iconic string sound that carries through 'Nosferatu'. Joe stumbled across the Chamberlin while recording at the Record Plant, and it is Joe himself who plays the Chamberlin on the recording.

Lyrically, the song is rather self-explanatory.

> *Deep in the heart of Germany*
> *Lucy clutched her breast in fear*
> *She heard a beat of her lover's heart*
> *For weeks she raved in dreams he appeared*
> *From far off Transylvania*
>
> *Only a woman can break his spell*
> *Pure in heart who will offer herself*
> *To Nosferatu*

After the first few verses and refrains that alternate between an oppressed atmosphere of gothic doom (verses) to a triumphant, anthemic quality (refrains) we arrive at a progressive mid-section where the guitars up their intensity and the lyrics again turn self-referential – compare 'Sickness now, then horrible death' to 'E.T.I.'s 'Sickness now, the hour of dread'.

The combination of the classically-tinged piano, the Chamberlin and the arcane subject matter, along with the symphonic form of the song, makes 'Nosferatu' vaguely reminiscent of another Pearlman/Krugman project, Missouri prog rockers Pavlov's Dog. The song ends with Donald playing a somewhat unusual solo where he veers close to David Gilmour's cinematic blues – a moving and majestic ending to an album rich in atmosphere but perhaps somewhat inconsistent in execution.

Considering the commercial aspirations the band and its producers had going into the studio, it must have been a disappointment, both for them and for Columbia Records, that the album failed to surpass, or even match, the sales of *Agents*. *Spectres* peaked at 43 on the Billboard albums chart, and the 'Godzilla' single, somewhat puzzlingly, failed to chart entirely. On the upside, the single got plenty of airplay and became an FM staple almost immediately. By the next year *Spectres* did manage to rack up sales for a gold disc, which was respectable, but still no match for *Agents'* platinum status.

Critics were more receptive to the band's commercial direction than audiences, ironically. John Milward, in his *Rolling Stone* review, was enamoured by the band's more mature approach, concluding that 'the Cult's creative combination of styles has pioneered a new genre of MOR heavy metal. Hard as nails but as sweet as cream, *Spectres* shows the Blue Öyster Cult to be the Fleetwood Mac of heavy metal.' That review must have made Sandy very happy.

The 2007 remastered and expanded edition of *Spectres* offered up four previously unreleased songs, most of them in fairly finished form. The pick of the litter is the band's enthusiastic cover of The Ronettes' 1963 hit single 'Be My Baby', the ultimate nod to Phil Spector, who produced the original. Joe had written a track that was originally called 'Dope Rider', which with some input from Donald eventually became 'Night Flyer'. It's a very complete song as it stands, and features a strong melody sung by Donald, and could have been a contender.

Donald's own 'Dial M for Murder' mixes a more classic BÖC sound, ca. *Secret Treaties*, with a nervous new wave energy. An interesting tune but probably not appropriate for the overall ambience of *Spectres*. Albert's 'Please Hold' is a retro-sounding '60s pastiche complete with twangy guitar, but not all that interesting musically.

Interestingly, an unreleased track from the previous album, Allen's 'Dance the Night Away', which appeared as a rough demo on the remastered version of that album, would have fit very nicely on *Spectres* had it been given the proper arrangement and production sheen.

In conclusion, *Spectres* is an album perched on a precipice – the band wanted to take one step further in the direction of the commercial success which *Agents* had afforded them. However, that step took them onto shaky ground. They were also not quite willing to make the full leap, meaning they had one foot still in their early '70s style and one foot in commercial mid-'70s rock. On the upside they got to further develop their pop smarts, but it appeared to come at the cost of that impressive consistency that had marked their previous albums. Maybe the old production magic from the triumvirate of Pearlman/Krugman/Lucas was not working as it should.

The man in white. Donald's image was a sort of antithesis to Eric's black leather in the 70s - he would usually appear in a white suit or outfit, as here in Copenhagen, 1975. *(Photo: Bolle Gregmar)*

LEFT: *Blue Öyster Cult*: Gawlik's black and white design evokes the architectural nightmares of H.P. Lovecraft. *(Columbia)*

RIGHT: *Tyranny and Mutation*: Gawlik was recommissioned for the band's second album, and outdid himself with this cosmic structure. *(Columbia)*

LEFT: *Secret Treaties:* Artist Ron Lesser, known for his characteristic work on posters for Western movies in the 70s, was commissioned to make the art for *Secret Treaties*, and delivered one of the most memorable covers. *(Columbia)*

RIGHT: The inner sleeve of *Secret Treaties* featured tantalizing hints to the *Imaginos* saga. *(Columbia)*

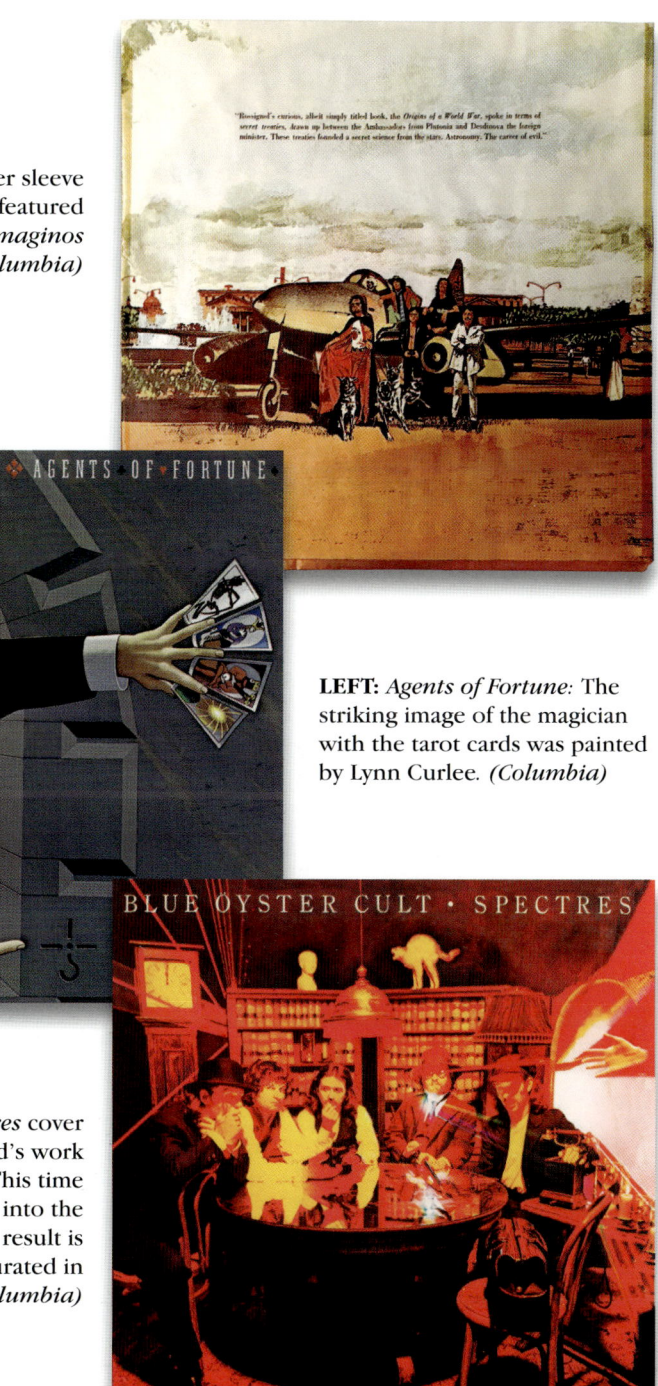

LEFT: *Agents of Fortune:* The striking image of the magician with the tarot cards was painted by Lynn Curlee. *(Columbia)*

RIGHT: The *Spectres* cover was a result of the band's work with lasers on stage. This time they brought the lasers into the photo studio, and the result is an ominous image saturated in red light. *(Columbia)*

LEFT: 'When I put that stuff on I felt like Batman.' A leather-clad Eric playing Copenhagen in Denmark, October 1975. *(Photo: Bolle Gregmar)*

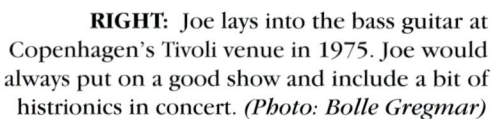

RIGHT: Joe lays into the bass guitar at Copenhagen's Tivoli venue in 1975. Joe would always put on a good show and include a bit of histrionics in concert. *(Photo: Bolle Gregmar)*

LEFT: Allen never stayed behind the keyboards for too long back in the 70s. He loved it best when he could strap on the guitar. Copenhagen, 1975. *(Photo: Bolle Gregmar)*

At certain points in concert, all members of Blue Öyster Cult will wield guitars. The fans know this moment as 'The 5 guitars'. Whether they all have such good taste in stockings as Albert, remains unknown. Their European tour in 1975 saw them at the height of their powers, touring the *Secret Treaties* album. Both a sonic and a visual assault! *(Photos: Bolle Gregmar)*

Above: The band in a publicity shot promoting the *Spectres* album. From the left: Donald 'Buck Dharma' Roeser, Eric Bloom, Albert Bouchard, Allen Lanier and Joe Bouchard. *(Columbia)*

Left: Eric Bloom relaxes between takes at the Record Plant, New York during the *Spectres* recordings, 1977. *(Photo: Modern Recording Magazine/ Lynn Goldsmith)*

Above: You can never go wrong with gang vocals. From the *Spectres* sessions. From the left: Joe Bouchard, Eric Bloom, Donald 'Buck Dharma' Roeser, Albert Bouchard, Allen Lanier. *(Photo: Modern Recording Magazine/Lynn Goldsmith)*

Below: Duelling guitars. Donald and Eric laying down tracks for *Spectres*. *(Photo: Modern Recording Magazine/Lynn Goldsmith)*

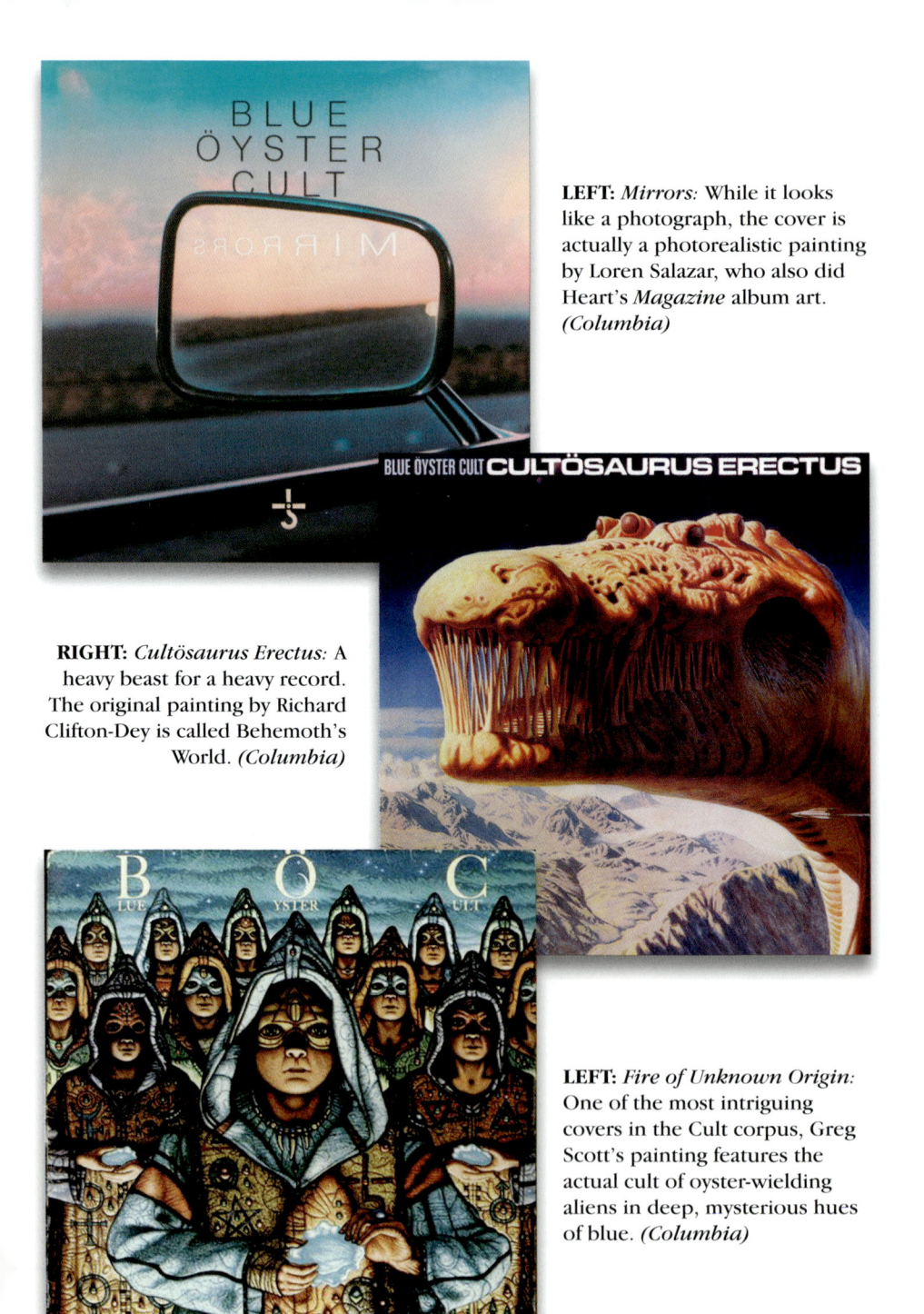

LEFT: *Mirrors:* While it looks like a photograph, the cover is actually a photorealistic painting by Loren Salazar, who also did Heart's *Magazine* album art. *(Columbia)*

RIGHT: *Cultösaurus Erectus:* A heavy beast for a heavy record. The original painting by Richard Clifton-Dey is called Behemoth's World. *(Columbia)*

LEFT: *Fire of Unknown Origin:* One of the most intriguing covers in the Cult corpus, Greg Scott's painting features the actual cult of oyster-wielding aliens in deep, mysterious hues of blue. *(Columbia)*

RIGHT: *Fire of Unknown Origin*, back cover: The ornately designed mandala originally appeared in a book about the occult, but artist Greg Scott thought it was appropriate for the album. *(Columbia)*

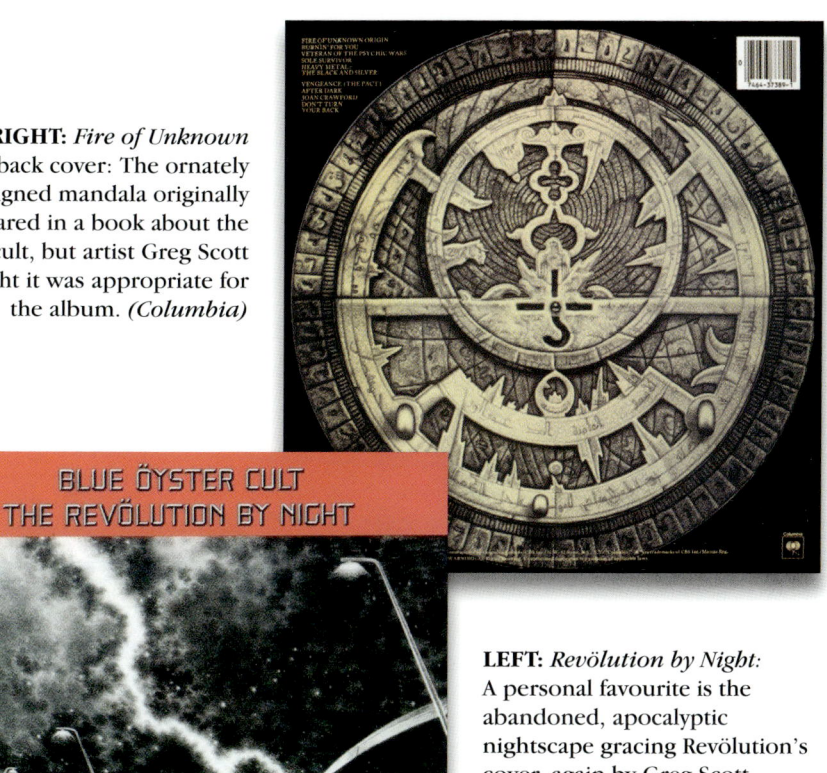

LEFT: *Revölution by Night*: A personal favourite is the abandoned, apocalyptic nightscape gracing Revölution's cover, again by Greg Scott. *(Columbia)*

RIGHT: *Club Ninja:* Many fans were taken aback by the less than subtle space opera art of this album. Art by Don Ivan Punchatz. *(Columbia)*

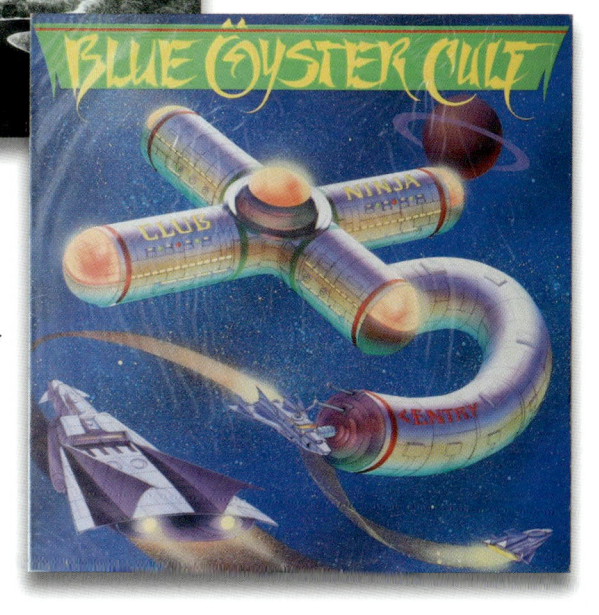

By the time *Spectres* was out, Blue Öyster Cult were already hard rock superstars. They toured the album in Europe as well, here on a Swedish stage in May, 1978. *(Photo: Bolle Gregmar)*

Donald in his classic white suit and sporting a sunburst Les Paul, in Sweden in 1978. *(Photo: Bolle Gregmar)*

The black and the white. Eric's 'Kronos' guitar is iconic, and he has had several made throughout the years. *(Photo: Bolle Gregmar)*

LEFT: *Imaginos:* Artist Greg Scott was originally commissioned to to the art for *Imaginos*, but in a last-second decision the label went with this haunting black & white photo, which turned out to be a good choice. *(Columbia)*

RIGHT: *Heaven Forbid:* 1998's comeback album originally featured a less than pleasant horror painting that was later replaced by this very un-Cultish glamour photo, making it look suspiciously like a Christian Rock release. *(CMC)*

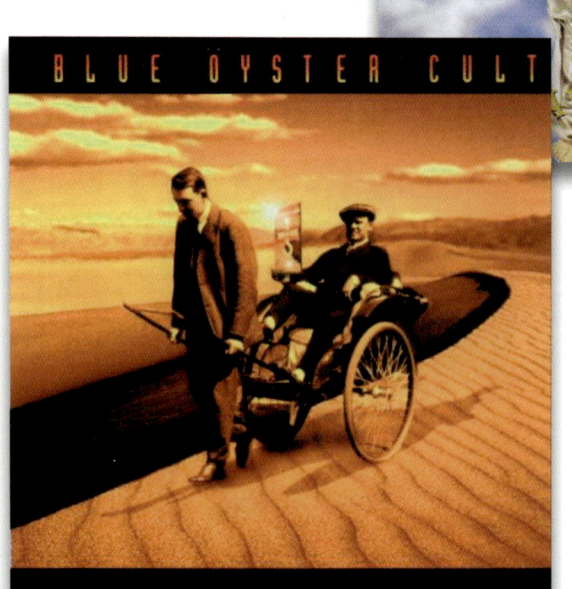

LEFT: *Curse of the Hidden Mirror:* After the unpopular cover for *Heaven Forbid*, the band made the wise move of commissioning renowned artist Ioannis for this cover, filled with Cultish clues. *(CMC)*

Above: Performing '(Don't Fear) The Reaper' at iHeartRadio in 2012. From left: Drummer Jules Radino, Eric Bloom, Donald 'Buck Dharma' Roeser and Kasim Sulton, known from the band Utopia.

Above: Donald and Eric are the sole remaining members of the original line-up, and keep the spirit of the Cult alive into the present day. Live performance at iHeartRadio.

Left: No pain, no gain. Columbia were fearless in their promotion of Blue Öyster Cult in the early days, and didn't shy away from S&M imagery or blasphemy. The template for a million 80s metal bands had been made. (Ad for *On Your Feet or On Your Knees*, 1975)

Right: Artist Todd Schorr painted the striking reaper image on the cover of 1978s live album *Some Enchanted Evening*. It was used in this ad for the album. Authors Terry Pratchett and Neil Gaiman famously referenced the cover art in their novel *Good Omens*.

Left: One of many bumper stickers that promoted Blue Öyster Cult in the 70s, perfect for that rockin' van.

Chapter 7: If you wanna face the music
Mirrors (Columbia 1979)
Personnel:
Eric Bloom: stun guitar, vocals
Donald "Buck Dharma" Roeser: lead guitar, vocals
Allen Lanier: keyboards, guitar
Joe Bouchard: bass, vocals
Albert Bouchard: drums, vocals
Additional musicians:
Mickey Raphael: harmonica on 'Dr. Music'
Jai Winding: strings on 'In Thee'
Ellen Foley, Genya Ravan, Wendy Webb: background vocals
Produced at Kendun Recorders, Burbank, California, CBS Recording Studios, New York City, The Record Plant, Los Angeles, California by Tom Werman
Release date: June, 1979
Highest chart places: 44 (US), 46 (UK)
Running time: 36:34

Mirrors is one of the most reviled albums in the Cult canon, often competing with *Club Ninja* for the place as the band's worst album, as judged by fans and heavy metal critics.

It may be time for a reappraisal of this often misunderstood album. If we take a step back and look at the previous album, the problem with *Spectres* was not the more commercial direction, but rather the fact that the band didn't quite have the guts to go the full mile. Some of the material was underdeveloped, and the production was stuck in the past – quite often on *Spectres* the enormous amounts of reverb and the lack of transient detail threaten to drown out the music.

From that perspective the band made a logical move by leaving their usual production team behind and hiring seasoned AOR producer Tom Werman. At the time, Werman was a hot producer at Columbia's subsidiary Epic Records, who had worked on successful albums by Ted Nugent, Mother's Finest, Molly Hatchet and especially Cheap Trick, a band the Öyster boys admired. Just like the Cult themselves, Werman appeared to operate in the borderland between pop and hard rock, and he seemed an obvious choice for a new album by a band that was still chasing that follow-up single to 'The Reaper'.

Opinions are divided on whether the gradual commercialisation of the Cult's sound in the late '70s was successful or not, and whether it was simply a kowtow to label pressure or a desired stylistic change within the band. However one sees it, one of the band's strengths has always been their extreme diversity, their ability to develop and even change styles without ever losing sight of that essential Cult-ness. It is a talent that is rare among hard rock bands. The only obvious comparison would be Rush, who transformed from Led Zeppelin-wannabees, via prog rock juggernauts to sleek '80s synth rockers without ever compromising their basic identity. Blue Öyster Cult is best understood in the same light.

But even for an eclectic band like the Cult, *Mirrors* may have pushed the stylistic envelope too far for many fans back in 1979, especially the fans who had followed the band since the heady early '70s.

However, with the benefit of hindsight, *Mirrors* stands as a fine example of that transition that most big '70s bands went through in the late '70s, a transition from quirky, progressive seekers to finely-tuned FM rock.

Tom Werman, who is known for mega-hits like Cheap Trick's 'Surrender', Mötley Crüe's 'Girls, Girls, Girls' and Ted Nugent's 'Cat Scratch Fever', took the basic recipe of the Cult's two previous albums and simply tightened it up and polished it. There was tension between Werman and Albert, as Werman wanted him to play tighter, simpler rhythms, whereas Albert valued his jazz swing. There was also friction with Eric, who by both his own and Werman's admission was somewhat side-lined during the recording. 'I honestly thought that Donald's voice was more appropriate for several of the songs that Eric had planned to sing', Werman told *Rock Candy* magazine (2018). 'I felt bad about telling him that, but I preferred to have the record come out better and Eric be pissed off, rather than please Eric and compromise on quality.'

With all due respect to Werman, the comment on quality is nonsensical as Eric is a virtuoso singer, just with a different style than Donald's. All the same, the album did end up being heavy on the Donald side. But ironically, the album also features some Eric highlights, as we shall see.

'Dr. Music' (J. Bouchard, Roeser, Meltzer)

From the first few seconds of the album it's clear that this is not your big brother's BÖC. 'Dr. Music' starts out with electronic moog drum fills and a funky bass line doubled by a bubbly synth bass. The drums have a clarity and openness that had not been heard on previous albums and yes, they are indeed very tight. Werman also applies his successful recipe of severely multitracking the central guitar riff to make it 'pop' or stand out in the mix. Another surprise comes in the virtuoso harmonica playing of guest musician Mickey Raphael, best known for his work with people like Willie Nelson and Townes van Zandt. In sum a whole new aural vista, for better or worse, unfolded before the listeners' ears when they put on *Mirrors*.

But as you get under the surface of the song and get used to the shiny sounds, you realise that it's still much the same old Cult. Joe wrote the better part of the song and provides some of his classic walking boogie bass, and Meltzer's lyrics tie in nicely with songs like 'The Red and the Black' and 'Dominance and Submission'.

Girl don't stop the screaming
You're sounding so sincere

So much beauty
In the tracks of your tears
So if you wanna face the music
Open up your ears
Meet my friend
Calamity Jane
Hear the rhythm
In the sound of her pain

It's a typical case of Cult subversion that such sordid and kinky penmanship is cloaked in glittering pop sounds.

'Dr. Music' demonstrates both the strengths and the weaknesses of *Mirrors*. Werman's production cuts away dead meat and shines a light on each individual instrument. Careful mixing ensures that no instruments mask each other. This is partly achieved by filtering out a lot of low end where it is not needed. That in turn creates more space for the fundament of the song, the kick drum and the bass guitar – essential focal points in a production from the disco-crazed late '70s. The upside is a tidy, clear and punchy sound. The downside is that you lose some of the meat, and also some of the harmonic interest that arises from instruments that overlap, frequency-wise. It is a difficult balance to strike. *Agents* was a rich, full and finely-honed production, a perfect example of mid-'70s production techniques. But on *Spectres* things got muddy – too much low end from too many instruments, and too much reverb obscuring the music. *Mirrors* is in some ways a natural counter-reaction to *Spectres*. You gain clarity, but you lose some warmth and substance.

'The Great Sun Jester' (Bloom, Michael Moorcock, John Trivers)

The up-tempo intensity of 'Dr. Music' is replaced by serenity when the 12-string acoustic guitar that carries 'The Great Sun Jester' arrives. A definitive album highlight, and one of Eric's finest songwriting contributions to the band, 'The Great Sun Jester' can only be described as a cosmic ballad, with lyrics by British science fiction/fantasy writer Michael Moorcock. This was the first of several collaborations between Eric, himself a huge SF fan, and Moorcock, who had already made a mark on the music scene through his collaboration with UK space rockers Hawkwind. The third contributor to the song is John Trivers, originally bass player in Eric's pre-BÖC band Lost and Found, later a member of Canadian pomp rockers Prism, today more known for his work with Tina Turner and for making the music to the famous Ridley Scott-directed Macintosh ad in the '80s. John and Eric would continue their co-writing relationship on several future Cult albums.

The song opens with the aforementioned 12-string guitar along with an organ-sounding keyboard and embellishments from a polysynth. The textures are reminiscent of prog rock or pomp rock balladry, closer in some ways to a band like Starcastle than to the Cult's murky past. The ethereal sound is befitting of Moorcock's tragic tale of a cosmic joker.

> *They have killed the Great Sun Jester*
> *Who danced between the stars*
> *They have stripped him of his manhood*
> *Signs of Venus and of Mars*
>
> *The cynics left him weeping*
> *And the jackals have left him torn*
> *And the Jester reaches out blind hands*
> *He can touch the stars*
> *No more*

The basic narrative is taken from an early Moorcock novel, *The Fireclown*, first published in 1965. A future world where people live underground has its hopes ignited, so to speak, by the eccentric savior figure of the Fireclown, the Great Sun Jester. Complications ensue, as they often do.

Eric's vocals are both passionate and sensitive in this song. Moorcock seems to always bring out an extra layer of emotionality in Eric. The drumming is also of notice, powerful but simple, but with some terrific whirlwind fills to build up the intensity and dynamics at strategic points in the song. Stylistically Albert's performance here points forward to the precise yet forceful drumming on the next two albums.

Allen plays quite extensively on the song, utilising thin, chorused string synthesiser sounds that are not prominent but serve to flesh out and widen the sound in an almost psycho-acoustic manner, a classic AOR production trick. The song ends with a fading coda that sees Donald deliver a very tasty, fleet-fingered solo.

'In Thee' (Lanier)

The next song is probably the best-known tune from the album and a bit of a miracle of pop writing. Surprisingly, it is not a Donald composition, but rather an Allen song. 'In Thee' is a departure from the usually funky sound from Allen's hands, instead it is a breezy, cool acoustic pop song carried by strummed acoustic guitars and effervescent 4-part vocal harmonies. Sung with an almost heartbreaking melancholy by Donald, the song seems to centre around the tribulations of long-distance relationships ('aeroplanes make strangers of us all').

Werman's delicate production touch really benefits 'In Thee'. The acoustic guitars are crisp and translucent, the vocal harmonies so tight and breezy they could make CSN jealous and the drums never get in the way of the song. Allen stays away from the spotlight, content to double the guitar chords with piano and fill out the soundstage with more of that string synth. Donald provides the occasional guitar fill before he gets a brief but wonderful solo after a few verses and refrains. That solo is pure melody and no showing-off, proving Donald could easily transition from hard rock guitar hero to more radio-friendly session-style guitar. After the solo the band falls away leaving just the simple organ chords and a single string synth note on top, an elegant simplicity reminiscent of The Cars, who the Cultsters admired at the time. Over this Donald provides some of his most intimate vocals, singing:

> *Once we breathed the breath of sweet surrender*
> *Pure, pure arab air filled our atmosphere*
> *But pride it makes stars of us all*
> *Until we fall*
> *For everyone to see*

Perhaps, like 'Goin' Thru the Motions', an indictment of the incompatibility of the touring lifestyle and relationships.

'In Thee' is a song that easily connects with listeners regardless of their relationship to the band, and it has proven to be a live favourite to this day. It was also the only single from the album that charted, cracking the Billboard Hot 100 and peaking at 74. Given more aggressive marketing, it is quite possible that 'In Thee' could have been a success on par with 'The Reaper' and 'Burnin' For You'.

'Mirrors' (Roeser, Bruce Abbott)

It is a little surprising that the band chose to pick the album's title from the song 'Mirrors'. It is hardly the most consequential or compelling song here, nor does it seem overly representative of the dominant themes on the record (love, loss and science fiction). 'Mirrors' is, like 'Golden Age of Leather', a co-write between Donald and Bruce Abbott. However, it lacks the epic grandeur of that song, both in music and words. An upbeat rock'n'pop tune carried on a somewhat stiff rhythm, the song starts nicely with harmony lead guitars before a less than exciting, if pleasant, progression and melody take over. Lyrically the song seems to condemn vanity, the female type in particular, which to modern ears is a little jarring and old-fashioned.

> *Pretty girls have a love affair*
> *With their eyes and their shining hair*
> *Fantasise that the world adores*
> *Tantalise like a cover girl*
>
> *Mirrors are the basis of beauty give rise*
> *To self-love or self-pity the prize*
> *If a woman is pretty she tries*
> *Like a superstar Hollywood girl*

It doesn't help when the chorus comes in, with its (probably intentionally) silly-sounding girl group choir of 'Pretty girls can't look away'. To put it bluntly, this song is a little beneath the band's usual intellectual standards.

'Moon Crazy' (J. Bouchard)

Thankfully side A is saved at the end by Joe Bouchard's brilliantly strange song 'Moon Crazy'. Inspired by Norman Mailer's *Of a Fire on the Moon* ('And Provincetown was like a province of the moon in these days of a moon-crazy summer'), 'Moon Crazy' is a little hard to describe. Led by piano and some trademark Joe bass lines, the song is also driven forward by Albert, who seems to have temporarily regained his swing and moves the song through several different rhythmic feels and time signatures. In some ways the song is close to the progressive pop/art rock scene that was blossoming in the late '70s with bands like City Boy and Supertramp. The chord progressions are unusual, with hints of jazz harmony and blues, and the song moves swiftly and effortlessly through several different sections. One highlight is an almost symphonic section with a stately Donald solo on top. The lyrics are also notable, penned by Joe himself and possessing an almost spectral quality.

> *Did you catch the fever*
> *Flying toward the moon*
> *Sailing in space to a distant shore*
> *You kind of wonder*
> *What they came here for*
>
> *We lived days for lovin'*
> *Falling for all we met*
> *A world gone crazy from the lunacy*
> *The tides kept rising and falling like you and me*

The drums are prominently mixed, with a thick, upfront snare sound that helps propel the song. Towards the end the drums kick into double-time, with additional handclaps and an almost gypsy-like solo from Donald, a quite memorable ending to side A.

'The Vigil' (Roeser, Sandra Roeser)

Side B opens with a fan favourite and the grand epic on the album, 'The Vigil'. A Donald-penned tune with lyrics from his wife Sandy, 'The Vigil' again picks up on the art rock feel of 'Moon Crazy' inasmuch as it is tighter and more concise than traditional progressive rock, but still packs plenty of complexity and is a multi-section song. The six and a half-minute journey contains some of Donald's finest guitar playing on the album, as well as remarkably clear and punchy guitar sounds. Albert's drumming is busy without being overwhelming, again with Werman's trademark punchy and well-separated sound. Donald provides both stunning lead vocal and those lush multi-part harmonies audiences had come to expect from him.

The song starts unusually with a lonesome acoustic guitar playing around an open A-string drone, before the band enters with lush, strummed acoustic guitars, lockstep drums and bass guitar and a languid lead guitar. Swirling sci-fi synth effects set the scene for the cosmic theme of the song. Then we switch to the central, heavy guitar riff that backs the verse sections.

In a purple vision
Many thousand years ago
I saw the silent stranger
Walk the earth alone

Twenty-seven faces
 With their eyes turned to the sky
I've got a camera
And an air-tight alibi

I know they're out there
We see them coming
Faster than the speed of light
They greet us in the dead of night

Classsic Cult theme, this, tying in with both older songs like 'E.T.I.' and future works like 'Take Me Away'. The 'twenty-seven faces' is probably a reference to the VLA, Very Large Array, a park of 27 radio telescopes watching the sky in New Mexico.

Around the three and a half-minute mark the music is stripped down to a single, strummed acoustic guitar and Donald ominously declaring 'I hear the whispers on the wind/They say the earth has fallen due'. This is followed by a very fast, picked guitar figure augmented and made more complex by rhythmic delay, a quite singular moment on the album and a bit of a showstopper in concert. A string synth sneaks in before the band and more vocals enter briefly. Then it becomes the backing for a very elegant solo from Donald with a smooth, rich guitar sound while foreboding bells and a deep choir intoning 'come to us' appear underneath it all. This is Blue Öyster Cult at its theatrical best.

The song then returns to the verse section before another guitar solo wraps it up. The coda is a return to the lonesome guitar that introduced the song, a nice dramaturgical touch.

'I Am the Storm' (J. Bouchard, Ronald Binder)
One might think that after this athletic exercise the band would settle down in a lighter groove but following 'The Vigil', we are actually treated to the album's

heaviest number, 'I Am the Storm'. While Joe wrote the music, the lyrics are the sole contribution to the Cult corpus by oddball character Ronald Binder.

Binder was known around the East Coast scene for being a bit of a hang-around, meeting up with favourite bands like Alice Cooper and The Dictators, running errands for the Cult and eventually forming a bond with Helen Wheeler, with whom, by his own admission, he was 'deeply in love'. He also became infamous for an incident where he 'leaked' Gene Simmons' actual Hebrew name to Kiss fans, allegedly as a revenge for Gene having bad-mouthed the Cult.

Binder delivered several lyrics to the band, but 'I Am the Storm' is the only one they actually used. Musically it is a song that hearkens back to earlier days, a heavy, up-tempo rocker with (finally!) some intense vocals from Eric, and Donald unleashing some of that frenetic hard rock energy he had withheld for most of the album. The music is descriptive of the megalomaniac lyrics:

Lightning bolts become my swords
When I pull them from the sky
Run my gauntlet of slashing rains
You won't survive to testify

When you see the clouds blacken
Remember you've been warned
No shelter from my fierce winds because
I am the storm

In many ways 'I Am the Storm' is a foreshadowing of the re-energised Blue Öyster Cult that appeared on *Cultösaurus Erectus* the next year.

'You're Not the One (I Was Looking For)' (A. Bouchard, Caryn Bouchard)

The album tapers off, for better or worse, with two softer numbers. 'You're Not the One (I Was Looking For)' was Albert's attempt to replicate The Cars. 'I took the Cars song, 'Just What I Needed', and put new lyrics to it', Albert told Martin Popoff (*Agents of Fortune*). It was intended as a joke, but the band went for it, to Albert's dismay. If nothing else, it's a fairly good pastiche, and shows that the band kept up with the new sounds of the late '70s.

'Lonely Teardrops' (Lanier)

'Lonely Teardrops', Allen's second song on the album, is a much more substantial and successful pop experiment. Starting off with a funky clavinet riff that carries most of the song, and backed by a slow disco beat, this is a gorgeous song with Donald singing the yearning melody with believable heartache.

Lonely teardrops you've been crying
I hear them fall
In the night the empty night
I hear your song
It goes right through me
It used to move me
Lonely, lonely

Lonely Paris, met a dancer
We did the stroll
Through the night the empty night
Four years ago
I thought she knew me
She gave it to me
Lonely, lonely

A particularly delectable part of the song are the sumptuous and sensuous female vocal harmonies, provided by Ellen Foley, Genya Ravan and Wendy Webb. Like 'Tenderloin' on *Agents*, this is an incredibly well-written song, flowing effortlessly and showing great emotional depth. That strain of sultry, nocturnal mystery that seems to lace most of Allen's writing is just as present here.

Mirrors would be the end of the line, at least for the time being, for the Cult's foray into lighter, commercial rock, a journey that had started with the inspiring success of 'The Reaper'. It may be a flawed album, and it is certainly patchy in places. On the other hand, it is the first Cult album with a truly consistent and polished production and, as I mentioned in connection with 'In Thee', it is easy to imagine that the catchier songs on the album could have ruled the airwaves given a better-planned promotional strategy for the label. As it was, Columbia didn't quite know what to do with the album, and only 'In Thee' charted. Within the band, opinions varied on the outcome. Eric was understandably dissatisfied, considering his diminished role on the album, while Donald and Joe in particular were satisfied with most of the outcome. As for producer Werman, he views the album as a positive experience despite its commercial failure: 'When I listen to *Mirrors* I am impressed by what we did together', he told *Rock Candy* magazine. 'There are quite a few moments where I am genuinely knocked out by what we came up with … I am happy overall. I think I rose to the occasion, and as far as I am concerned, if Donald liked it, then I'm delighted.'

Now, in the name of rectifying some false history, *Mirrors* was not the complete commercial bust that some writers would have it. It peaked at #44 on the Billboard 200, the same placement as the preceding live album *Some Enchanted Evening*, which was considered a success, and only one step behind *Spectres* (#43). It may not have had the smash hit that *Agents* did, but for an experimental hard rock band already eight albums into their career I would hardly call it a complete failure. However, many fans felt alienated by the increasingly soft sound of the once-menacing Cult, and critics too felt that something was awry. Rolling Stone disliked the album and ended their review with the salty line 'For Blue Öyster Cult, it's time to fear The Reaper'.

No doubt, it was time for the Öyster boys to shake things up and to regain their mojo.

Chapter 8: New worlds waiting in the skies
Cultösaurus Erectus (Columbia 1980)

Personnel:
Eric Bloom: guitar, keyboards, vocals
Donald 'Buck Dharma' Roeser: lead guitar, bass (on 'Deadline'), keyboards, vocals
Allen Lanier: keyboards, guitar
Joe Bouchard: bass, vocals
Albert Bouchard: drums, vocals
Additional musicians:
Don Kirshner: introduction for 'The Marshall Plan'
Mark Rivera: saxophone
Produced at Kingdom Sound Studios, New York by Martin Birch
Release date: June 1980
Highest chart places: 34 (US), 12 (UK)
Running time: 41:10

For all its shiny production and individually strong songs, *Mirrors* was a disappointment, both to the label, to the band, and to the band's inventor. Pearlman was deeply dissatisfied with *Mirrors*. He had recently taken over managerial duties for Black Sabbath and was aware of producer Martin Birch's gargantuan effort to reinvigorate and reinvent the now Dio-led Sabbath. All the Öyster boys had great admiration for Birch through his work on the classic Deep Purple albums, so it was agreed to bring Birch onboard for an album that everyone understood must be a return to a heavier, stranger sound. The Blue Öyster Cult were in search of their roots.

The choice of Martin Birch as producer proved to be a success on several levels. His laidback approach, and his long experience in dealing with hard-rocking bands with strong personalities made him a perfect fit for the Cult. Unlike Werman, he often deferred to the band's preferences and took a back-seat approach until his help was called for. According to Eric, 'Martin Birch is a great guy. I don't know how we got him to produce – I think it was through our management – but we really enjoyed working with him. He was a bit of a madman, one of the boys, but super cool to deal with. Lots of fun.' (Interview with Musicradar)

For Eric the album was a return to form personally as well. He sings lead on six of the album's nine songs and brought some of his best writing to the table with 'Black Blade' and 'Lips in the Hills'.

For Albert, much was at stake with *Cultösaurus Erectus*. Like Bloom, he had found the *Mirrors* experience depressing and he was clear that the band needed to get back to what they were good at. 'We were trying to get back to our eclectic and almost annoying habit of not being pigeon-holed by anyone.', Albert said in an interview with *Deep Cut Classic Rock*.

The band holed up in Long Island's Kingdom Sound studio with Birch and worked intensively on what was again a collection of songs that mostly came out of the band's home studio demos.

'Black Blade' (Bloom, John Trivers, Michael Moorcock)

The ball opens with 'Black Blade'. Like 'The Great Sun Jester' this is a collaboration between Eric, John Trivers and Michael Moorcock. From the outset it is clear that heaviness has returned with a vengeance. Swirling sci-fi synth effects preface the main riff, delivered with crushing guitars and a loud, mean drum kit heavy on kick and toms and light on fluff. This was the heaviest the band had sounded since *Secret Treaties*, and due to increased audio fidelity maybe even heavier. As the band settles into the slightly quieter groove of the verses, carried by a Purple-sque octave-alternating guitar, Eric sings the tale of Moorcock's tragic hero Elric, doomed to fight a cosmic battle for eternity, forever bound to his magical, sentient sword Stormbringer, the Black Blade, who always craves new souls. Hawkwind did of course make an entire album about Elric and his sword (*The Chronicle of the Black Sword*), but in many ways Eric's more progressive approach is a better fit for the ornate and philosophical atmosphere of Moorcock's Elric books. Running at six and a half minutes, 'Black Blade' is a definitive return to the Cult's most adventurous '70s moments.

The chorus has Eric screaming 'It howls, it howls like hell', referring to Elric's 'singing sword', and he really embodies Elric's torment. The voice is treated to a flanging effect making it sound slightly alien and futuristic. In the verses we gain insight into Elric's tormented existence as a slave to his sword.

> *I'm told it's my duty to fight against the law*
> *That wizardry's my trade, and I was born to wade through gore*
> *I just want to be a lover, not a red-eyed screaming ghoul*
> *I wish it'd picked another to be its killing tool*

After some vocal sections the music dies down to a muted staccato guitar that then builds in intensity before it expands into an instrumental reiteration of the chorus with a brief but wild guitar solo. This is interrupted by an almost prog metal breakdown with unison runs between bass and guitar and bursts of Hammond organ, before the fiery guitar solo resumes. After another unison breakdown the band settles into a slow two-chord vamp where we are treated to a Joe bass solo. Anyone who heard the Cult in the '70s and '80s knew that Joe could deliver some mean bass solos, but we never got one on album, except for a brief fill on 'Godzilla'. But here he stretches out a bit, nothing showy, but very appropriate, and it functions as a perfect transition to yet another section of the song. Synthesiser chords and synth bass along with bass guitar dominate as feedback tones from a tortured guitar wind their way through a tense but pretty progression, creating a suspenseful science fiction atmosphere before the verse returns, this time with just a lone synth and Eric sounding agonised as he sings 'There's death from the beginning, 'til the end of time'.

After the chorus explodes for a few final rounds another futuristic synth sounds the last transition, a double-time groove overlaid by Eric on a creepy vocoder taking the character of the evil sword itself, ending on this depressive note:

> My master is my slave
> Ha ha ha ha ha ha…
> You poor fucking humans

'Monsters' (A. Bouchard, Caryn Bouchard)

There's no letting go as Stormbringer's last words die out and we get a new, relentless riff from 'Monsters'. Albert wrote the tune, with words from his wife Caryn, and we get clear echoes of Albert's early '70s King Crimson fascination, as the central riff is a quickfire guitar/sax unison theme that could have belonged on one of the early Crimson albums. The verse that follows is very heavy indeed, with incredibly forceful, bona fide metal vocals from Eric. It's easy to hear Martin Birch's production hand here, with his experience from British metal production.

What's less expected are the sudden breaks into pure jazz! Out of the blue Albert swings it up, Joe switches to a pure walking bass, Allen pounds out old-school jazz chords on the piano and Billy Joel saxophonist Mark Rivera takes the spotlight with a riveting sax solo.

The carousel swings around one more time, with more heavy verses. It's not entirely clear what the narrative is, but space travel is a definite element.

> Got our hands on a ship
> And stole away into the night
> The four of us and Pasha dear
> She to steer and we to fight
>
> Fed up with rules and regulations
> No more laughter left on Earth
> Outer Space our one salvation
> May God help us in our search

The jazz returns, this time with audience noise as if we're in a crowded jazz club. And, not to be outdone by 'Black Blade', 'Monsters' shifts gears yet again, into another unison riff even more reminiscent of 'Schizoid' Crimson riffage, complete with some militaristic snare playing from Albert. The tension of the riff resolves in an almost pastoral section with reverberated piano and guitar chords floating around in a way that is almost reminiscent of the most serene moments of fusion groups like Mahavishnu Orchestra and Return to Forever. And if all that wasn't enough, Albert has held out on the refrain of the song all the way until the end. Insanely catchy, the chorus of 'monsters, monsters' is an echo of the final chorus section of 'Astronomy', to the extent that one suspects Albert of being consciously self-referential here. Donald delivers a wonderful solo over the fading choruses where he plays off his own rhythmic delay effects.

'Divine Wind' (Roeser)

Things calm down somewhat, although they don't necessarily get less heavy, on the downtempo, sepulchral 'Divine Wind'. A fan favourite written by Donald but sung by Eric, the song is a rare political statement from the band, criticizing Iran's Ayatollah Khomeini in the wake of the Iranian hostage crisis. The slow tempo of the song and the minor key riff brings the song almost into Sabbath-esque territory, but not quite. Donald steers clear of power chord clichés, instead opting for more sophisticated harmonisations and an open, spacious arrangement that is more Pink Floyd than Black Sabbath. 'Divine Wind' is a truly remarkable song, steeped in atmosphere and with a hypnotic groove. Eric also delivers a pinnacle vocal performance here, sounding so forceful, yet controlled. The anger as he sings 'If he really thinks we're the devil, then let's send him to hell!' (a reference to Khomeini's description of the USA as 'The Great Satan') is palpable. Donald juxtaposes images of American and Iranian life in the lyrics, for example:

Fast food, fast cars
Fast women, movie stars
Time of trouble, time of trial
Turn to Memphis, pray a while
If he really thinks we're the devil
Then let's send him to hell

The rhythmic foundation is a slow shuffle held by Albert while Joe sticks to a simple, bluesy bass riff except for the ascending chords of the choruses. Allen is central to *Divine Wind* with what sounds like a Prophet 5 synthesiser providing both atmospheric string sounds and choral textures. Guitaristically speaking, this is the standout track on the album, with Donald totally unleashing his inner David Gilmour with long, sweeping lines and a dark, bluesy feel. Donald, who tends to stick to the higher registers when soloing, allows himself to explore deeper pitches in his leads here, further underlining the sombre ambience of the song. Especially the final solo is a soaring statement, with some wonderful drum fills from Albert as well. All in all, 'Divine Wind' is probably one of Donald's most weighty and serious contributions to the band.

'Deadline' (Roeser)

Side A ends with another Donald song, this one in a much lighter and poppier vein. A bouncy, bendy bassline underscores an up-tempo pop song made extra attractive by glimmering, ear-candy synths and a cheerful strummed acoustic guitar. This is classic Donald catchiness, and as expected he also takes the lead here. His vocals somehow manage to straddle the lightness of the music and the downright macabre content of the lyrics.

> *You said you'd be here at a quarter to five*
> *I didn't know if you were dead or alive*
> *How long you think that I can sharpen my knife*
> *I've got better things to do with my life*
>
> *It's almost the deadline*
> *Don't miss the deadline, darling*
> *When all your bad dreams will come true*

Again, one has to marvel at the Cult's ability to sugar-coat the actual story of their songs in inviting sounds. Subversion seems to be their middle name.

'Deadline' is not the most consequential song on the album, but it is the obligatory Buck Dharma pop excursion, and a nice one at that.

'The Marshall Plan' (Bloom, A. Bouchard, J. Bouchard, Lanier, Roeser)

Side B opens very controversially with two songs that many fans have a problem with. 'The Marshall Plan', a collaborative writing project involving the whole band, is a rare moment in the Cult's history where they lose their cool and the scale tips from tongue in cheek to banal humour. It's a song that may have worked better in the hands of rock humourists like The Tubes or early Meat Loaf, but it honestly falls flat on its face on a record that is supposed to be the Cult's heavy, sinister re-entry on the metal scene. A musically bland hard rock song, the lyrics tell the tale of Johnny whose girl is lured away by rock stars at a concert, and to win her back he realises he has to become a rock star himself. A spoken word section of the song goes like this:

> *Boy, if I only had a good guitar and a big amp*
> *Boy, wouldn't be somebody else taking my girl away…tell ya*

We are a long, long way away from the alchemical wordplay of 'Flaming Telepaths'. 'The Marshall Plan' is one of the biggest missteps in the band's history. Granted, there are musical bits that are good – Donald does a good arena rock impression during his/Johnny's guitar solo. But the premise of the song is unworthy of the Cult, and 'The Marshall Plan' is best forgotten.

'Hungry Boys' (A. Bouchard, Caryn Bouchard)

Rather unnervingly, things do not improve as we skip to the next song. In fact, Albert and Caryn Bouchard's 'Hungry Boys' has none of the redeeming qualities of the preceding song and goes down in history as the single worst

Blue Öyster Cult song ever. It is very difficult to understand what the intention behind this song was, and why it was ever considered for inclusion on an album that for the most part is impeccably Cultish. My best description of the song is that it sounds like a Zappa pastiche of cock rock, but without the humour and without the musicianship. And the lyrics ... this is the chorus:

We're hungry boys!
We're hungry boys!
We're hungry boys!
We're hungry boys!
Hungry, hungry, hungry, hungry boys!

The fact that the subject matter – addiction – is actually a serious one, makes the silliness of the song even more unforgivable. We better skip, yet again, to the next song.

'Fallen Angel' (J. Bouchard, Helen Wheels)

Thankfully, as they often do, the Oyster boys have saved some of the best for last. Joe's 'Fallen Angel', written with Helen Wheels, is in many ways a perfect sequel to 'Celestial the Queen', both in subject matter and musically. The song starts with some grandiose, suspended chords before a very Styx-like pumping groove enters and Allen plays some deliciously pompy moog embellishments over urgent, soaring chords. The music is immediately engaging, but the real revelation is Joe's vocals. I've always liked his vocals, that have tended to have a frail vulnerability to them. But here Joe throws caution to the wind and belts it out like he was the born hard rock singer! It sounds like he's discovered vocal resources he never knew he had. The juxtaposition of the relatively complex, semi-proggy arrangement of the song and Joe's hoarse, forceful vocals works very well indeed. Like most of Helen's lyrics this one straddles the worldly and the celestial realms.

From the dust I rose on high
Thunder cloud in a two-lane sky
From the world I did rebel
A fallen angel

Highway lust was in my blood
No girl could ever take my love
Cold and cruel and then I fell
A fallen angel

When Joe delivers the lung-emptying line 'Gonna rise up from hell', it's the kind of moment that makes your hair stand up.

After an interlude of bubbling synth arpeggios Donald delivers a short but perfect guitar solo, benefitting from the fact that the song is in a tempo that seems to be ideal for his playing technique. Joe's own appreciation for this song is clear from the fact that he has both re-recorded it for a Helen Wheels tribute album, and also done a 'rave' remix of it.

The album ends with my two personal favourite songs on the album. While songs like 'Black Blade' and 'Monsters' are indeed heavy and great songs in their own right, they do miss that element of the surreal that really makes Cult songs, well, Cultish. But with 'Lips in the Hills' and 'Unknown Tongue' all the weirdness of the 'Black and White' period comes rushing back.

'Lips in the Hills' (Bloom, Roeser, Meltzer)

'Lips in the Hills', written by Donald and Eric and with lyrics by Richard Meltzer, starts with a fast, distorted guitar ostinato before power chords come crashing in along with the band. Both the fast pace and the abrasive guitar sound makes this not only the heaviest song on the album, but the one closest to actual heavy metal. In fact, the sound is not a million miles away from the New Wave of British Heavy Metal, a sound Martin Birch himself was instrumental in creating through his subsequent work with Iron Maiden.

The verses take us back to the boogie sound of the first two BÖC albums, but this is boogie on testosterone, with thick, chunky layers of guitars. An extended pre-chorus with a rumbling bass and string synth filling out the soundstage builds tension before the iconic chorus of 'Lips in the hills', an image only Richard Meltzer could come up with. One theory about the lyrics is that they deal with the Roswell incident, but I think these words are very open to interpretation.

Up in the sky
Beyond the chasm
My eyes behold
A rare phantasm
The Godless night, the night that I saw
Lips in the hills

Over the bed of boogie Donald takes a bluesy guitar solo that is a clear echo of the style he employed on *Tyranny and Mutation*, but with added dexterity and grit. 'Lips in the Hills' is an exhilarating ride that successfully fuses the esoteric hard rock of the band's past with the re-energised approach that Martin Birch brought to the table.

'Unknown Tongue' (A. Bouchard, David Roter)

The strangest, and most evocative song on this album is without a doubt Albert's 'Unknown Tongue', a co-write with his friend, comedian and musician David Roter. Cleverly arranged to accommodate both heavy guitars and a dramatic, classically infused piano from Allen, the song picks up a bit of the art-rock vibe from *Mirrors*, but with a lot more weight to it thanks to Birch's production. The words supposedly relate to a friend of David Roter's, a 'nice Catholic girl' with a habit of cutting herself and drinking her own blood. True or not, the lyrics are striking, and whether they are seen as a tale of vampiric self-mutilation or of sexual awakening they certainly add some lurid mystery to the proceedings.

She put her hands upon her breasts
And they were small and hard and young
And everywhere she touched she felt a fire
Waiting for the answer that must surely come
Is this the way to love
Or is this just the way to die?

Speak to me in many voices
Make them all sound like one
Let me see your sacred mysteries
Reveal to me the unknown tongue

The chorus contains both some fine vocal harmonies and some clever rhythmic wrongfooting from the mischievous Albert. Midways we get to hear a bit of a piano solo from Allen – how we have missed that – with cool boogie-woogie lines before another verse takes everything down. Allen plays some tense, fast piano arpeggios that are punctuated by bursts from the rhythm section as Eric, with restrained menace, sings:

Then she took her father's razor
And watched it cut into her palm
She put her hand up to her mouth
To taste the blood so holy and warm

This almost horror movie-like vibe is a fitting ending to an album that thematically seems to deal with monsters both external and internal.

Cultösaurus Erectus is a bit of an odd entry into the Cult discography. It is incredibly well-produced and may contain the band's finest playing on a studio album. It also contains a wealth of strong material, displaying both a burgeoning '80s metal sensibility and a connection to the band's 'classic' past. However, the two enormous missteps opening side B rob the album of some of its magical aura. It is also really only towards the end of the album that you get that strong sense of the old BÖC mojo.

Still, there is no doubt that *Cultösaurus* was exactly the strong, hard-hitting comeback album the boys had hoped for, and the choice of Martin Birch as producer seemed to have been the right move. He provided plenty of punch and brought out an almost virtuoso feel from the musicians. Critics appreciated the return to form, with the UK's *Melody Maker* declaring: 'The Cult are still going strong with ex-Sabbath producer Martin Birch forging a brisk sound to match their mighty dynamics'.

Sales-wise there was a slight, if not ground-breaking lift, with the album staying in the Billboard Top 200 for 16 weeks, peaking at 34, their highest position since *Agents of Fortune*. More significantly the album did very well in the UK where it climbed to number 12 in the album charts. The combination of Martin Birch's British hard rock credentials and the local rebirth of metal through the New Wave of British Heavy Metal meant that the UK was fertile soil for Blue Öyster Cult at the time. The 'Fallen Angel' '45 also received decent airplay on the British Isles.

Some final words about the artwork of *Cultösaurus*. The cover painting is by SF artist Richard Clifton-Dey. It is not a specially commissioned piece but one the band came across and thought was appropriate, and indeed it is. The back cover is quite entertaining, picking up on the crypto-zoological bent of the album's title. Pictures of excavated dinosaur remains are captioned with a litany of in-jokes, from the 'Museum of Diz-Bustology' to 'professor Victor von Pearlman'.

The Cult were back, and the stage was set nicely for their next, mystical venture.

Chapter 9: Home in the darkness
Fire of Unknown Origin (Columbia 1981)
Personnel:
Eric Bloom: vocals, guitar, bass on track 5
Donald 'Buck Dharma' Roeser: lead guitar, vocals, percussion on track 3, bass and sound effects on track 8
Allen Lanier: keyboards
Joe Bouchard: bass, vocals
Albert Bouchard: drums, synthesiser, vocals, mixing (uncredited)[4]
Additional musicians:
Karla DeVito: background vocals on track 4
Sandy Jean: background vocals on track 9
Bill Civitella, Tony Cedrone: additional percussion on track 3
Jesse Levy: string arrangements on tracks 3 and 8
Produced at Kingdom Sound Studios, New York and The Automatt, California, 1981 by Martin Birch
Release date: July 1981
Highest chart places: 24 (US), 29 (UK)
Running time: 39:06

The experience of working with Martin Birch, and the response from both fans and critics to *Cultösaurus Erectus*, gave Blue Öyster Cult a shot in the arm. Although internally the band was at this point fraught with tensions, especially focused on what some in the band saw as increasingly erratic behaviour from Albert, there was still a sense that they could capitalise on the momentum of *Cultösaurus* and make an even better record. Ironically, Albert was the one who by his own account felt particularly invested in the album, despite some personal problems both with substance abuse and his love life. 'I really worked hard to try and make everybody else's stuff sound great, to the point of living in the studio. Of course, I was getting a divorce, so I was in no rush to go home, but I just stayed in the studio for three months while we made that record and worked with Martin Birch' (Interview with *Classicbands.com*)

To many members of the band the album stands out as one of their favourites. Eric, who contributed a lot of songwriting to the album and sings lead on all but three songs, loves the album. 'I think any BÖC fan would salute this record. We've got 'Burnin' For You', another big hit. Buck took lyrics from Richard Meltzer and turned it into a song. It has the same chord progression – B-A-G – as many tunes, including '(Don't Fear) The Reaper', but it sounds totally different. It clicked. I wrote 'Veteran Of The Psychic Wars', which got picked up for the *Heavy Metal* movie, so I got lucky there. 'Joan Crawford' has a great piano by Allen – it was a live mainstay for us for many, many years. *Fire of Unknown Origin* was another gold record for us.' (*Musicradar*)

The band returned to Kingdom Sound studios after having worked on material since January 1981 at the See Factor rehearsal studios. With Martin Birch back behind the console, everyone was excited by the material, and hopes were high for the outcome.

'Fire of Unknown Origin' (Bloom, J. Bouchard, A. Bouchard, Roeser, Patti Smith)

The album kicks off with a Patti Smith lyric the band had considered for inclusion on both *Agents* and *Spectres*, then with a different musical backing. This time, 'Fire of Unknown Origin' finally came to fruition over a new musical bed from Albert. In a contemporary radio interview with Jim Ladd, Eric light-heartedly – or candidly – explained the general process of writing, where everyone comes together at someone's house to listen to each other's recent demos and 'tell everybody what asswipes they were for writing such disgusting songs', and how one of these meetings left him with a particular tape in the car.

> *'I was driving somewhere, and I had this composite tape, and I thought I might as well listen to this stuff ... I get to one of these songs, it's just a track, no lyrics. And it reminded me of 'Riders on the Storm', just in the bassline. I had always wanted to, as a matter of fact I had a home demo that I had made two years ago, of 'Fire of Unknown Origin' with the feel of 'Riders on the Storm'. That's the way I thought the song always should be. So I told Albert, that track you wrote, with that bassline, why don't we try to put the 'Fire of Unknown Origin' lyrics over that, and he said, great idea!'*

It's an interesting peek into the songwriting process of a song that had a long gestation process, went through several versions, but because Patti Smith's lyrics were so obviously well-fitted to the Cult, they never gave up. It's also interesting that 'Riders on the Storm' pops up yet again as an inspiration for the band.

And sure enough, after a synth heavy intro that in fact sets the stage for the Cult's most synth-dominated album to that date, the 'Riders' bassline does enter as the main underpinning of the verses. Later in the song there are even synth embellishments that echo Ray Manzarek's 'raindrop' electric piano lines. Guitar and polysynth chords carry the harmonic content of the verses, panned to opposite sides of the bass guitar. It becomes clear from the beginning that Birch made a conscious decision to push Allen's synths forward on this album, something that adds to the mysterious atmosphere of the album and adds a tremendous amount of colour and texture compared to the more guitar-dominated *Cultösaurus*. Eric sings his melody with a laidback maturity that impresses. The self-confidence of the band at this point was evident – there was no need for the musicians to show off or assert their egos.

The chorus is relatively simple, but effective, with some interesting voicings from Allen's synth. The whole song in fact flirts with non-rock harmonics with an abundance of major and minor 7ths and inverted voicings.

After the second chorus round, a descending chord progression enters, overlaid by a beautiful harmonised guitar melody that evolves into a brief guitar solo before the verse enters again. The lyrics seem to be a perfect amalgamation of Patti Smith weirdness and the band's increasing preoccupation with alien visitations.

Swept her up and off my wavelength
Swallowed her up
Like the ocean in a fire
So thick and grey

A fire of unknown origin
Took my baby away
A fire of unknown origin
Took my baby away

The song eventually fades out with those Manzarek-referencing synth raindrops falling over the verse progression. 'Fire of Unknown Origin' is a somewhat unassuming, but incredibly atmospheric and mood-setting opener to the album.

'Burnin' For You' (Roeser, Meltzer)

'Fire' is followed by the second most important song in the Cult's career, 'Burnin' For You'. Starting life as a song intended for Donald's solo album *Flat Out*, the song eventually made it into the Cult oeuvre with a Richard Meltzer lyric. It was not obvious that it was going to be on the album. Donald wanted to keep it away from the band, and Joe had his misgivings about its appropriateness as a Cult song. But after Joe and Albert had worked a bit on the rhythm track to heavy it up, it was decided that it was a strong contender for radio play. As it turned out, 'Burnin'' became the band's second major hit single, making it to a staggering no. 1 on the US rock charts and enjoying world-wide airplay to this day. It has amassed a similar legacy to 'The Reaper', having been covered by diverse artists like power metallers Iced Earth, punk musician Mike Watt and Elvis Presley's daughter Lisa Marie, and it has also appeared in several movie soundtracks.

As Eric pointed out, it shares a similar chord structure to 'The Reaper', but it feels quite different, more like a power pop-meets-arena rock song that wouldn't have been out of place on one of Cheap Trick's more commercial albums.

The song starts off with a nimble, little guitar melody over a slightly off-kilter kick and snare from Albert before the sound widens in scope to encompass the song's signature wordless choir of richly harmonised aaahs, Albert's clever tom/snare pattern that almost works as a melodic counterpoint to the rest of the music, and Donald's soaring guitar lead. The widescreen sound is almost symphonic in nature and must have been a bit of a revelation for radio listeners back in the day. It was the kind of clever ear candy more often associated with producers like Robert 'Mutt' Lange and mega-budget bands like The Cars and Foreigner.

It doesn't hurt the impact of the song that the words by Meltzer are his most coherent and relatable. The verses arrive with a stripped-down semi-reggae groove with choppy rhythm guitar running through a delay effect in the right channel and an insistent, propulsive bass from Joe. Over this Donald sings a succinct melody made up of short, almost conversational phrases that allow for plenty of breathing space for the rest of the music.

The lyrics employ repetition as an effective poetic tool in a text that is part Jack Kerouac's *On the Road*, part love song and part Ecclesiastes ('To every thing there is a season, and a time to every purpose under the heaven').

Home in the darkness
Home on the highway
Home isn't my way
Home I'll never be

Burn out the day
Burn out the night
I can't see no reason to put up a fight
I'm living for giving the devil his due
And I'm burnin', I'm burnin', I'm burnin' for you

Time is the essence
Time is the season
Time ain't no reason
Got no time to slow

'Richard would write on a typewriter', Donald told *The Herald Tribune* in a 2017 interview. 'And we'd have sheets of lyrics and on the page and it would look just look like poetry with a lot of lower case and free form, free association. I don't know how long I'd had his lyric, but it was about 1980 and we'd moved to Connecticut. Originally it was going to be on my solo record, but Sandy convinced me to give to BÖC. I wrote it in my garage studio. I'm quite proud of it. It's one of Richard's more sentimental lyrics, something he's not known for'.

A lengthy pre-chorus prefaces the actual chorus, all sung with impeccable cool and detachment by a Donald who is right in the pocket of the moment of this song. The instrumental section on the bed of heavenly vocal harmonies returns for a brief, melodic solo before the vocal sections resume. A longer guitar solo follows, where Donald pulls out all of his best tricks, using harmonics, double-stops and bends, all with an almost funky feel that must've made a young Prince jealous. The song ends with the 10cc-like vocal harmonies doubled by a power chord.

In some ways 'Burnin' For You' was the culmination of every lesson Donald had learnt writing pop songs for the Cult, and once the label heard it they must have known they had a hit on their hands.

'Veteran of the Psychic Wars' (Bloom, Moorcock, Trivers)

From the bright FM sound of 'Burnin'' we enter a much darker territory on Eric's 'Veteran of the Psychic Wars'. Another co-write with Moorcock and old bandmate Trivers, this is one of the most monumental and intense of Cult's songs, and possibly the finest of all of Eric's vocal performances. The slow tempo, the orchestral percussion, the bowed double bass and the astral synthesisers all add up to a sound unlike anything else heard on a Blue Öyster Cult album.

The song starts with slow, martial percussion, the result of several band members and others playing what sounds like floor toms in the studio, and sombre synthesiser chords. A 9th floats around the basic Eb chord in the beginning, creating a sense of unsettled suspense. A bowed double bass comes in to fill out the bottom, while a cello sneaks in over it, setting up the orchestral sound before the verse settles the song in its home chord of G minor. The verses really only consist of a bleak synth progression of descending chords and those martial drums, over which Eric spins Moorcock's tale of a veteran of a futuristic war. While the concept seems abstract, both Moorcock's words and Eric's vocal delivery makes it feel stirring and intimate.

> *You see me now a veteran of a thousand psychic wars*
> *I've been living on the edge so long*
> *Where the winds of limbo roar*
> *And I'm young enough to look at*
> *And far too old to see*
> *All the scars are on the inside*
> *I'm not sure that there's anything left to me*
>
> *Don't let these shakes go on*
> *It's time we had a break from it*
> *It's time we had some leave*

The lyrics are a tie-in with Moorcock's tales of eternal, cosmic war, where many protagonists, including the aforementioned Elric, are avatars of a single archetype, the Eternal Champion who must forever fight in a cosmic battle between Order and Chaos.

The bleak atmosphere continues throughout the song, where the synths are occasionally joined by dark, lingering guitar chords and sinuous lines from the double bass and cello. The restrained but gothic, neo-classical arrangement and the insistent, deep percussion reminds one of the kinds of sounds that would come out of experimental acts like Dead Can Dance and This Mortal Coil later in the decade.

During the choruses Eric really embodies the pain the everlasting war has caused the eternal warrior as he pleads: 'Oh please, don't let these shakes go on!'

'Veteran' also features one of Donald's most remarkable solos. Playing off a long delay tail, he starts out by playing short phrases and leaving room for the delay to repeat them over the stark, electronic backing, before he builds a harmony out of the overlapping echoes. It's the kind of economical but emotionally striking approach usually associated with guitarists like The Police's Andy Summers or Rush's Alex Lifeson, and it serves the song perfectly. The solo climaxes with militaristic bursts on the snare drum and synths emulating orchestral stabs. The song returns to the atmospheric vocal sections before ending in an epic crescendo of strings, synths and drums. Veteran is also a live favourite for the band and is usually expanded with a more rock-based instrumental section in double-time. To this day it remains an iconic BÖC composition that to fans and casual listeners alike exemplify the mysterious sci-fi aura surrounding the band.

'Sole Survivor' (Bloom, Liz Myers, John Trivers)

Fire of Unknown Origin is in some ways a tripartite work, where the three first songs are the standout, high profile tracks, and the last three tracks are the 'deep cuts'. The middle three, however, constitute a slight low point.

This middle section starts well enough with Eric's 'last man on earth' fantasy 'Sole Survivor'. It is another co-write with John Trivers, but also with Trivers' wife Liz Myers, best known for having co-written the Eddie Money hit 'Shakin''. With both Trivers' and Myers' AOR credentials it's not surprising that 'Sole Survivor' also sounds a bit arena rock – in addition to sharing its title with an Asia song. It starts very elegantly with a cool, jazzy bass line and a hi-hat and nothing else, until a thick, chorused synth pad, presumably played either on a Prophet 5 or an Oberheim OBX, creeps in underneath. Then enters the verse, where the bass changes up into something minimalist and funky, while the otherworldly synths remain. Eric sings with restraint and melancholy over the stripped down, almost new wave-like backing. A picture is painted of a lonely man in a hopeless predicament.

> *There walked a lonely man*
> *Silent, mute the only man*
> *Not knowing how, not knowing why*
> *Was he the sole survivor?*
> *Why should he be alive*
> *Breathing still while others died*
> *And the only question*
> *Why was he the sole survivor?*

The chorus is where the slight corporate rock feel creeps in. It is based around a tried-and-true i-VI-VII-v progression (you'll find it in Bon Jovi's 'It's My Life' for instance) that seems a little too generic for the Cult's usual tastes. Thankfully things are improved by a Hammond organ doubling the guitars, giving us a whiff of that *Secret Treaties* sound, as well as some tasteful female backing vocals. As the verse re-enters I personally experience a dissonance between the synth-laced, cool moodiness of the verse sections and the workmanlike nature of the chorus. Much is redeemed however, by Donald's brief but efficient solo, which features heavy use of the whammy bar, somewhat unusually for Donald. The haunting glissando notes fit well with Allen's ominous synths.

Apart from some space invader synth effects and more whammy bar licks, not much more happens in the song. The ending is a protracted, slowly fading repeat of the rather stiff-legged chorus.

'Heavy Metal: The Black and Silver' (Bloom, A. Bouchard, Pearlman)

'Heavy Metal: The Black and Silver' is an odd one. One of three songs on the album specifically written for the *Heavy Metal* soundtrack, it is the only song on *Fire* to feature a Sandy Pearlman lyric. The basis for the song was an Albert tune called 'Ear Damage', from which they borrowed the main riff. Then Sandy, Albert and Eric worked on the lyrics, which in reality are basically a cut-up of phrases borrowed from an astronomy book, Adrian Berry's *The Iron Sun: Crossing the Universe Through Black Holes*.

According to Eric in the radio interview with Jim Ladd, 'Pearlman walks in with this treatise on black holes (...) Neutron stars and the Einstein Bridge and all these things that Sandy's into, the esoterica of *Scientific American* which he reads religiously (...) Albert took it and pulled out the best lines and tried to write a song with it, and we were still like only 50 percent of the way there. And then Albert turns it over to me and says, here, you try it. Then I took it (...) and made it about 80 percent there. And then me and Sandy and Albert sat down and picked each other's brains for about a half hour and finished it up'.

In other words, this song is not directly linked to the *Imaginos* cycle. Musically it's a bit of a head-scratcher, rather simplistic and blunt for a BÖC song. It starts with abrasive guitar feedback before the overdriven riff enters. Apocryphally, the rhythm guitar is played by Albert, although he is not credited. Eric is, however, credited with bass since the band liked his feel when he played bass on the track. The vocal melody was more or less ad-libbed by Eric in the studio, which is not surprising once you hear it. It works well enough though, and Eric interjects some faux-passion to the otherwise rather nonsensical lyrics.

A notable aspect of the mix in this song is that while it is de rigeur in guitar-heavy music to use a noise gate on distorted electric guitars to suppress the noise that wells up between played notes and chords, it is not used here. In between each chord that Albert or Donald plays, there is a burst of noisy feedback that adds a bit of a live and 'out of control' feeling to the song. While 'Heavy Metal: The Black and Silver' has to be considered more pastiche than serious song entry, it is nevertheless an entertaining end to side A.

'Vengeance (The Pact)' (J. Bouchard, A. Bouchard)

Side B begins with a typical Joe epic. 'Vengeance (The Pact)' is another song that was submitted (but not used) for the *Heavy Metal* movie. It started life as more of a humorous tune named 'Dakota Silo Sitter', a story about a guy, apparently an eskimo, that Joe had met whose job it was to sit watch over a nuclear silo in Dakota. The only problem was that he was a very nervous and fidgety guy, a 'pencil eater', which Joe figured would make for a funny song. Brother Albert thought differently. According to Joe: 'Musically I had figured how 'Morning Final' and 'Nosferatu' had been my two epic sounding songs, and this was to be the third in the series, with elaborate chord and tempo changes. Not your typical candidate for a hit song. I played the song to Albert who thought the track was great, but said, 'Let's get rid of this Eskimo story,' and he began writing the new lyric straight out of the script from the *Heavy Metal* movie.' (*Morning Final* #14)

The song starts out with sequenced synthesiser before it's joined by a minor key guitar riff. The verse has Joe doing his best heavy metal voice, the lyrics sounding out like a battle cry atop a bed of chugging, rhythmic guitars.

> *See them standing in the foothills*
> *Waiting for the kill*
> *On wings of fear the terror sweeps*
> *Into the city beat*

The chorus has Donald joining in on lush harmony vocals, adding a bit of that AOR feel, while Joe provides some memorable bass lines underneath.

Being a Joe song, this one goes through a few changes, the first being a section with a particularly pristine Donald solo over a bed of string synthesisers, Donald employing a crystal clear but overdriven sound for his lead. The following vocal section also has a gravity-defying feel to it, even though the lyrics signal a downfall:

> *Close my eyes*
> *And I am there*
> *I feel I'm falling down in a deep, dark pit*

The next transition is highly unusual, as Albert keeps a simple drum groove over a minimalist backing and gradually increases the tempo – the only instance I can think of in the band's catalogue where a gradual tempo change is employed. As he settles into a new, faster groove, the band comes in with one of the most metal moments in the band's history, a galloping, Iron Maiden-like riff with Joe shouting out lyrics describing some of the *Heavy Metal* movie's more dramatic action. Eventually the song returns to its original tempo and a repeat of the chorus before the song ends with a spaced-out synth effect. 'Vengeance' is not Joe's best epic, but it does fit in well with the general mixture of science fiction and sword & sorcery on the album, and the cinematic air of a lot of the songs.

'After Dark' (Bloom, Liz Myers, Trivers)
We arrive now at the third part of the album, the deep cuts, if you will. First out is an Eric tune, and a bit of an undervalued piece of BÖC real estate. 'After Dark' is co-written with John Trivers and his wife Liz Myers, but unlike 'Sole Survivor' this is not generic-sounding at all. An up-tempo pop tune with a dark feel to it, it starts with fast, nervous drums and an up-front bass augmented by new wave synths and guitars. It's nice to hear Eric sing some slightly lighter material after all the intensity of *Cultösaurus* and most of this album too. The chorus is especially cool, where Eric doubles himself with a deep octave, giving extra gravity to the lyrics:

> *Long ago and far away I heard your voice*
> *Once I heard you sing your song I had no choice*
> *Terror took control, it told me what to say*
> *And let me loose, I fear I've finally found a way*

It's yet another tale of vampirism, but you can never get enough of those when you get Eric singing immortal lines like:

> *There's no turning back now*
> *My fate is traced in blood*
> *I've tasted true salvation*
> *Your power is my drug*

The song also features a solo from Donald where he really lets loose. It starts with some fierce tremolo-picking, maybe a nod to his surf guitar heroes like Dick Dale, and continues with his most up-tempo and playful guitar work on the album. The tightness and energy of all the players here shows that 'After Dark' was a song they all enjoyed playing. There's a touch of the virtuoso prog pop of *Mirrors* here, a tinge of The Cars, but wrapped up in the darkly luminous shadings of the rest of the material on *Fire of Unknown Origin*.

The song ends on a histrionic howl from Eric – boy can he hit those upper registers – before a final instrumental flurry punctuates the song.

'Joan Crawford' (A. Bouchard, Jack Rigg, David Roter)
A total textural shift occurs with the next song. After almost an entire album where Allen has stuck exclusively with synthesisers and keyboards, 'Joan Crawford' opens with gorgeously played classical piano complete with romantic flurries and more than a little bit of inspiration from Grieg's *Piano Concerto in A minor*. It's almost baffling to hear this from Allen, whose instrumental presence in the band is usually very subtle and restrained, but here Lanier the Pianist really steps forward. After a last, descending crescendo of piano notes, the band kicks in with some precise punches while the piano lays into a swift arpeggio, before the verses take over.

'Joan Crawford' is one of the band's magnum opuses in my estimation. Some have criticized it for its 'silly' horror movie lyrics, but we are after all talking about Blue Öyster Cult. The lyrics were by Albert's buddy David Roter, the one who wrote the equally disturbing 'Unknown Tongue', while Albert wrote the song with some arrangement input from another friend, Jack Rigg. Joe, being the band's only classically trained musician, contributed to some of the piano parts.

Joe: 'Working out the piano part on 'Joan Crawford' was a fun experience. Albert had me play classical-style piano parts over and over in my garage, and he took the tapes and edited them together and then Allen added some of his stuff to it. I remember doing this on the day John Lennon died, kind of eerie to look back on it like that.' (*Morning Final #14*).

The lyrics are partly inspired by Joan Crawford's daughter Christina's sensational tell-it-all *Mummy Dearest*, which was made into a movie the same year *Fire* was released, revealing her mother's dark and abusive side. The song's lyrics are a creepy, surreal mélange of zombie horror, sadomasochistic Catholic school girls and apocalyptic street scenes.

> *Junkies down in Brooklyn are going crazy*
> *They're laughing just like hungry dogs in the street*
> *Policemen are hiding behind the skirts of little girls*
> *Their eyes have turned the colour of frozen meat*
>
> *No, no, no, no*
> *No, no, no, no, no, no, no, no*
> *Joan Crawford has risen from the grave*

One of the band's more outrageous music videos was made for this song. Blue Öyster Cult had a fairly decent presence on early MTV and were one of the earlier hard rock bands to really get a grip on music videos. But this particular video, every bit as kinky and weird as the song, was too much for MTV, who banned it.

Musically this is also a high point on the album, Eric being the perfect vocal oracle for all things creepy. His performance here is second only to 'Veteran of the Psychic Wars', and he also has good melodic material to work with. In many ways 'Joan Crawford' is a precursor to the epic, storytelling songs Albert wrote for the *Imaginos* cycle, all stormy drama and theatrical moves. At the same time Birch's production really shines here, providing room for everything without ever getting cluttered. The drums are dynamic and clear without the overly compressed sound that affected *Cultösaurus*. Little touches like the cello that enters in the second verse, and the amazing sound effect cut-up that creates an entire movie in the head halfway through the song, do so much to enhance the atmosphere. Towards the end comes the scariest part of the record, as a muted guitar and bass pulsate beneath Albert whispering 'Christina, mother's home … come to mother'… Spine-chilling stuff. Another entertaining production detail is the quote from *The Hall of the Mountain King* – also from Grieg's *Concerto in A minor*, during the final choruses.

'Don't Turn Your Back' (Lanier, A. Bouchard, Roeser)

There is no pause as Eric sounds his final warning about Joan the zombie. A hi-hat flutters briefly before a little tom run takes us into the last song on the album, 'Don't Turn Your Back'. Allen's last songwriting contribution to the band, it is also one of the most refined compositions on the album. Donald helped out with the lyrics, borrowing imagery from the *Heavy Metal* movie, and he also made some melodic contributions. But, basically this is Allen's baby and has his trademark subdued, melancholy mood and subtly funky feel. The song is carried by lush synthesiser chords, a lively, bouncy bass line from Joe and Albert's grooviest playing on the album. After minimising his swing and syncopations on most of this album and the previous two in the name of hard rock rigidity, the groove is back in the form of a gentle shuffle. Donald gets the lead vocal, and rightly so, as the yearning melody is right up his alley.

The lyrics work well even without knowing the movie for which they were written. As in 'Burnin'', repetition is used as a hypnotic device, while the words paint a picture of impending but hidden danger.

Don't turn your back
Danger surrounds you
Don't turn your back
To the dogs who hound you
Don't turn your back
Don't show your profile
You'll never know
When it's your turn to go

A middle section is underpinned by a Motown-derived bass ostinato and shimmering synths while Donald weaves one of his typically effortless and elegant melodic solos on top. This segues into a vocal bridge that is also very trademark Donald, all airy harmonies, before the song returns to its foundational verse and chorus. 'Don't Turn Your Back' is both a poignant and enchanting end to Allen's writing contributions to the band, and a perfect encapsulation of the record's mysterious and mature sound. It is also a worthy exit for Albert, for whom *Fire of Unknown Origin* would be his last album with the band.

Fire of Unknown Origin is not the easiest album to rank in the Cult discography. It is first and foremost a continuation and a maturation of the new-found energy and focus the band found on *Cultösaurus*. But where *Cultösaurus* felt a little bit like the Cult trying to be a 'real' hard rock band rather than their chaotic, eclectic selves, *Fire of Unknown Origin* really lets the band be who they are. Producer Martin Birch obviously found his groove with the band here and allows the music both more dynamism and space and more colour. The coloration from Allen's rich synthesiser palette is especially noteworthy, as is the forceful but natural drum sound on the album.

Additionally, and unlike *Cultösaurus*, *Fire* contains some of the band's strongest and most iconic material since *Agents*, in the form of songs like 'Burnin' For You', 'Veteran of the Psychic Wars' and live favourite 'Joan Crawford'. However, the one thing that keeps the album from climbing into the very upmost echelons of the Cult's oeuvre, is its unevenness. The middle three songs, while not as glaringly annoying as the previous album's 'Marshall Plan' and 'Hungry Boys', are a little too generic – uncharacteristically lacking in character, so to speak – compared to the sharp writing on the rest of the album. So, while it is tempting to proclaim the album a complete winner, one can only do so with that caveat.

It probably didn't matter much to the band or the label, who must have been thrilled to finally have a Top 40 hit again. 'Burnin' For You' was released as a single that not only spent three weeks in the Top 40 of Billboard's Hot 100 chart, it also reached an incredible #1 on the Billboard Mainstream Rock chart. The song was everywhere on FM radio, and just like 'The Reaper', the single pulled the album along with it in the charts. The album peaked at #24 on the Billboard 200 and it also did well in the UK, entering the Top 40 there.

The album was a critical success as well, with even highly mainstream media like *People* Magazine ('The Cult proves melody and hard rock are not mutually exclusive') taking notice. *Rolling Stone's* Parke Puterbaugh wrote: '*Fire of Unknown Origin* is potent hard rock informed by literate songwriting, assured ensemble playing and flawless production.'

Blue Öyster Cult were now riding the crest of their second commercial wave, but as the subsequent touring began, it would become clear that the internal chemistry of the band was not quite as solid as their recent album.

Before we move on to the next phase of the band, a quick word on the cover. Fans must have taken notice of artist Greg Scott's cover painting for *Fire*. Painted in luminous and otherworldly shades of blue, and indeed depicting a cult of oyster-wielding aliens, it was clear to the initiated that this was actually a picture of the Blue Öyster Cult itself. Greg Scott worked as the art director for

Rolling Stone and was already familiar with the band – was in fact a huge fan. He really hit a home-run with his painting for *Fire*, which would initiate a new, three-album visual era for the band, just like the 'Black and White' era, and just as effective.

Chapter 10: At the clover-leaf junction
The Revölution by Night (Columbia, 1983)
Personnel:
Eric Bloom: guitar, vocals
Donald 'Buck Dharma' Roeser: lead guitar, keyboards, vocals
Allen Lanier: piano, keyboards
Joe Bouchard: bass, electric and acoustic guitars, vocoder, vocals
Rick Downey: drums
Additional musicians:
Larry Fast: synthesisers, programming
Aldo Nova: guitar and synthesisers on 'Take Me Away'
Gregg Winter: backing vocals on 'Eyes on Fire'
Randy Jackson: bass on 'Shooting Shark'
Marc Baum: saxophone on 'Shooting Shark'
Produced at Boogie Hotel Studios, New York, Kingdom Sound Studios, New York and The Automatt – Studio C, California by Bruce Fairbarn
Release date: November 1983
Highest chart places: 93 (US), 95 (UK)
Running time: 41:44

With the band on a serious roll, there was time for some heavy-duty touring in the wake of *Fire of Unknown Origin*. The tour, which also took in Europe, was documented on the double live album *Extraterrestrial Live* (more on that in the live album appendix). But during the tour, the schism between Albert and the rest of the band widened to the point where something had to give. It was Albert who had to give in the end. He was replaced mid-tour by drum roadie and lighting designer Rick Downey. The exact reasons for the conflict are beyond the scope of this book; suffice it to say that Albert made some bad life-style choices, missed a few shows and generally had gotten on the nerves of his band buddies for a few years. In some ways it was probably for the best for all parties. The Cult got some new blood and fresh incentive, and Albert was free to concentrate on the *Imaginos* project.

Revölution by Night, the first Blue Öyster Cult record to feature a non-original member, is in some ways the Cult's 'Canadian' album. Canada was at the forefront of high-tech, melodic hard rock at the time with bands like Rush, Saga and artists like Aldo Nova making inroads in the US as well.

Based on his successful work with another Canadian hit group, Loverboy, the Cult decided to work with Canuck producer Bruce Fairbairn. When he prematurely passed away in 1999 he left behind a legacy of platinum classics like Bon Jovi's *Slippery When Wet* and Aerosmith's *Permanent Vacation*. Interestingly, Fairbairn started his career in music as a trumpetist with a fusion band that later metamorphosed into Prism, the very same pomp rock group that would later feature Eric's good friend and co-writer John Trivers. Another friend of Eric's, and also Canadian, Aldo Nova helped out both with songwriting and playing on the album. Other guest appearances included highly respected synthesiser pioneer Larry Fast (known for his work with Peter Gabriel) and session bass player (and American Idol personality) Randy Jackson, who would later help Journey out with their double platinum Raised on Radio.

No shortage of talent, in other words.

In spite of the considerable forces involved in making the album, many fans see the album as a disappointment, especially coming on the heels of *Fire of Unknown Origin*. Some consider it too slick, too electronic sounding or too commercial. But the album was at the same time both a logical next step in the band's evolution and also a very successful bridging of the old and the new. There are more links to the 'Black and White' period on *The Revölution by Night* than on any of the previous three albums, and there is also a return to some of the goth and gloom that characterised '70s Cult music – and would fully re-appear with a vengeance on *Imaginos* a few years later. It's possible that the production trappings of the album – the electronic drums, the shiny, synthetic textures and the bright, digital reverbs – occlude the fact that most of the songwriting really is good, old-fashioned Cult stuff.

The band went into the Boogie Hotel, a renowned recording facility in Jefferson Port, NY, to record. Albert happened to be working on *Imaginos* in the same studio complex, so they would frequently be running into each other. Additional recordings were done at their old haunt Kingdom Sound, and at the Automatt in San Francisco where Randy Jackson overdubbed his parts.

'Take Me Away' (Bloom, Aldo Nova)

The Revölution by Night storms out of the gates with Eric and Aldo's 'Take Me Away'. Bright, brash drums, a hooky guitar riff and Eric showing off his poppier side as singer, all signal a new take on the Cult sound. In some ways this song sounds like it could have been written by Donald. In fact, the music is written by Aldo Nova, whose lite-metal-meets-pop solo albums are not, in fact, a million miles away from Donald's compositional style. Eric provided the lyrics, a classic exploration of his favourite theme: extraterrestrial visitations. It's quite a personal take on his obsession, where he pleadingly asks the visitors to bring him with them.

> *Fantasy fills my mind*
> *To leave this place before my time*
> *Release myself from earthly care*
> *My dream may be your nightmare*
>
> *I turn my hopes up to the sky*
> *I'd like to know before I die*
> *Memories will slowly fade*
> *I lift my eyes and say*
> *Come on take me away*

The chorus is indisputably catchy, and the listener finds herself immediately empathising with Eric's earthbound prayers. A notable detail in the choruses is the use of Simmons electronic drums for the tom fills. It was perhaps not the wisest production choice, the sound being thin and synthetic, but at the time Simmons drums were 'the shit' and showed that the producer was hip to the latest gear.

After the second round of choruses the music hushes down into a cosmic foray into electronics that sounds positively Teutonic, all blips and beeps and synthetic carpets of sounds that may be a combination of Aldo's and Larry Fast's input. This break culminates in a bright-sounding and intense solo from Donald, showing that he could compete with the best of the new generation of '80s guitar heroes. This again is followed by some fiery unison runs affirming that connection with the Cult of old, before the vocal sections resume. The song ends with another tight unison flurry.

'Take Me Away' would turn out to be a well-deserved sleeper hit with FM radio, and also had a very entertaining music video made to it. As an opening to *Revölution*, 'Take Me Away' showed that fans need not worry that the Cult was losing their steam – here was plenty of energy.

'Eyes on Fire' (Gregg Winter)

But older fans may instead have started to worry by track 2, 'Eyes on Fire'. The first Blue Öyster Cult song not to have any writing input from members of the band, it was written by Gregg Winter, a Long Island songwriter who gave a cassette of the song to Eric. Gregg's main claim to fame outside of having written for the Cult, was as a producer/songwriter for Swedish melodic rockers Treat, a band of modest international success that were forever doomed to live in the shadow of Europe (the band, not the continent). Interestingly, Treat recorded their own version of 'Eyes on Fire' on their 1986 album *The Pleasure Principle*. It has a harder-edged production and a different bridge, but the verses and chorus are the same.

For BÖC, it was probably the most purely AOR song the band has ever recorded. It was chosen for submission to the album because Eric enjoyed singing it, and one can understand why. It has a pleasantly soaring melody that you could hear a Lou Gramm or a Steve Perry tackling. It's a good showcase for Eric's more soulful side as a vocalist. The song starts with a Journey-like piano doubled by a subtle string synth, before a pumping post-disco beat enters to back the verses and continues through the anthemic chorus. The lyrics are not really your typical BÖC fare; it seems to be the lament of a guy who is being 'friend-zoned' by the girl he loves:

> She thinks I'm sweet and gentle
> She thinks the world of me
> But late at night I'm not the one she needs
> She never looks at me

> *With eyes on fire*
> *Glowing like coals in the night*
> *Hungry eyes*
> *Burning with love and desire*

A very far cry from cosmic conspiracies and alchemical secrets. Still, the song works well enough in context and is not nearly as offensive as some fans would have it. The boys manage to inject some Cultish moments into it via some tasteful guitar work and Eric's voice which sneaks in a pinch of darkness to elevate the song from its generic roots.

'Shooting Shark' (Roeser, Patti Smith)

While 'Eyes on Fire' may be a slight hitch in the momentum promised by 'Take Me Away', things are set right again by the one song from the album that most fans agree is a bona fide classic: Donald's 'Shooting Shark'.

An epic, labyrinthine tale of love, magic and prophecy, the lyrics were penned by Patti Smith and was one of those poems Donald had lying around for years before he made a song out of it. Donald: 'We never actually wrote songs together as an intentional project, what we would do is Patti would give us a lyric or we would go in her book of writings and take a section of something and create songs from it. When I wrote 'Shooting Shark' I hadn't seen Patti in seven, eight years, after she left Allen and married Fred 'Sonic' Smith. I came across the typewritten sheet and went, 'Wow, this has been here all along.' So I created the music from the words. There wasn't actually much direct interaction.' (Interview, *Popentertainment*)

It is unclear from the lyrics exactly what a shooting shark is, but the narrative appears to be about someone who is trying to get over/get away from a lover and gets advice from a soothsayer or magician.

> *Well I bumped inside the magic man*
> *And he laid some tricks on me*
> *He said, 'You do need help, my friend'*
> *I whispered, 'Obviously'*
> *He laid a spread of Jacks and Queens*
> *And he bade me take my pick*
> *But every face it had your face*
> *I cried out, 'I am sick'*
>
> *Sick of hauling your love around*
> *Want to run the train alone*
> *But the engine tracks straight through your heart*
> *And weighs me like a stone*

The song starts very unusually for a Cult track, with a lone drum machine playing a programmed pattern. It is then joined by another uncharacteristic sound from the band, a slap-hand bass line. The slap bass is actually played by Randy Jackson, the above-mentioned session legend. The bass propels the song, along with the basic drum pattern that remains throughout the song, augmented by human-played drums as well. The synths arrive along with the bass, a combination of scintillating pads and cavernous bass surges. The entire aural presentation is cinematic in scope, and I was not surprised to see this song included on a list of 'songs that should have been played on *Miami Vice* but weren't' on a *Miami Vice* fan site. It has that neon-drenched moodiness that characterised the music in that show.

While the electronic soundscape and the funky feel, courtesy of the slap bass, may be new territory for the Cult, it retains its band identity through Donald's voice and guitar. The central verse has a strong melodic profile and plays off the underlying rhythms, coming in on an off-beat to accentuate the syncopated feel of the basic beat. The chorus widens the soundstage with wordless vocal harmonies and added layers of keyboard, over which Donald sings a particularly yearning and almost mournful melody of exquisite beauty. It is clear that the composer took pains with this song, as everything seems to be maximised for full emotional impact. Donald himself often mentions this song as one of his favourite 'deep tracks' from BÖC.

The song has a cyclical structure, alternating between verses and choruses without too much variation in the arrangement, which creates a hypnotic effect and focuses the attention on the unfolding story in the lyrics. The vocal sections are punctuated by succinct guitar fills. At the very end however, we are treated to a surprising but somehow wholly appropriate saxophone solo by Marc Baum. His previous credits included stints with disco star Sylvester, and this is definitely a solo on the pop side things, adding even more of that *Miami Vice* feel. A colourful ending to a centrepiece song on the album.

'Veins' (Roeser, Meltzer)

Interestingly, the band chose to put another storytelling Donald song at the end of side A. In 'Veins' Donald uses lyrics from Richard Meltzer, an unusually linear and lucid piece of storytelling for him. The protagonist wakes up to the angst-filled notion that he has become a murderer.

> *I open my eyes*
> *From a dreamless night*
> *With a sense of dread*
> *You could cut with a knife*
> *So I'm thinking that*
> *Maybe I killed somebody*
> *You never know—you never know when*
> *You might have killed somebody*

Veins in my eyeballs
Damage that I've done
Veins on the stairway
Veins in my skull

Notice the references to older BÖC lyrics towards the end there.

The song opens with majestic synth – Donald had acquired his own Prophet 5 synth at this point and wrote this song on it – before more electronic drums and a driving guitar riff joins the fray. The song has an urgent, runaway feel to it which fits the lyrics to a tee. There is even a breathless quality to Donald's vocal melodies that underlines the nightmarish scenario of the lyrics, even though the song still remains within the same pop metal boundaries as 'Shooting Shark'. During the pre-chorus and chorus there are repeating single chord stabs from the synth and guitar that almost sound like alarms going off. Midways through the song Donald puts in a brief but ferocious and raw guitar solo before the song climaxes with the narrator's realisation that yes, he did indeed kill someone, and the song ends with a siren-like synth and the electronic drums.

The hi-tech sheen, the orchestral synthesisers and the tense atmosphere of the song brings 'Veins' in line with certain late-period pomp rock acts like California's under-recognised White Sister, who also experimented with new technology in their emotion-packed rock. And just like White Sister's songs tended to pop up in '80s teen horror flicks, 'Veins' would have been perfect as background music in a John Carpenter movie.

'Shadow of California' (J. Bouchard, Pearlman, Neal Smith)

As we move on to side B of *Revölution by Night*, it's worth reminding ourselves that this album was recorded next door to Albert's *Imaginos* sessions. This meant that both Albert and Sandy were back in the Cult's orbit. The track that kicks off side B is 'Shadow of California', a very substantial dip back into the Pearlman universe, and specifically the 'Transmaniacon MC' timeline of his mythology. The origins of the song seem a little muddled, but it is believed that the song is related to one of the unreleased *Imaginos* tracks, 'Half-Time Life'. Written by Joe Bouchard in collaboration with Alice Cooper drummer Neal Smith (who he would soon be working with in several post-BÖC projects including Deadringer), the Pearlman lyrics bring this song right into the fold of the band's classic early '70s work.

Both the album's title and the artwork are inspired by the lyrics of this pivotal track. An attempt at an interpretation of meaning would go something like this: The 'revolution by night' is Pearlman's alchemical, transformative revolution of rock, a destructive force to lay waste the current order of things, as laid out in older lyrics like 'Transmaniacon MC' and 'Cities on Flame With Rock and Roll'. In 'Shadow of California' the riders from the Transmaniacon Motorcycle Club, agents of revolutionary change, have time-travelled to a future California, ultimate destination Los Angeles, where they have come to wreak havoc – and revolution – like the Four Horsemen of the Apocalypse.

Beneath the freeway at the cloverleaf junction
A symbol of good luck emanates darkness
The shadow will grow to cover California
Somewhere on the road from San Bernadino
Its future is stirring the past...will not pass

Speed is the game in this shadow of kings
Where the company of Angels fly
They appear at the crossroads at once in the future
Clad in the darkness on the highways of night
With no love....from the past

Night makes right
The symbol remains
Into the darkness
Must pour the brains
In the Shadow of California

The song starts with heavy power chords backed by high-pitched synths and again the Simmons toms. I have seen that both band members themselves and critics keep singling out the Simmons drums as the major failing of the album. While I don't think it is the greatest sound in the world, I have to admit that I see it differently. The electronic drum sounds fit the generally tech-ified sound of the album well. I think we have also come to a point in time when the most 'dated' '80s sounds that used to embarrass us, now have gained a nostalgic sheen and have become hallmarks of an era of production that we can admit to remembering with some fondness.

The verse is carried atop a staccato bass/guitar riff with nods to the *Peter Gunn* theme that moves through what is basically a blues progression. As befits the heaviest song on the album so far, Eric takes the lead vocal and gives us some of that '70s grit that has so far been missing from the album. His vocal is shadowed by a vocoder-like effect which along with shimmering synth chords lend the verses a futuristic feel. In many ways 'Shadow of California' delivers the best of both worlds – Eric in his intense hard rock mode, heavy riffing based on a modified blues and Pearlman's cosmic lyrics all point backwards to albums like *Secret Treaties*, while the mechanic rhythms, the effervescent synths and the vocal treatment scream the 1980s.

The chorus bursts out of the speakers with walls of vocal harmonies, tremulous synth strains and Eric approaching the histrionic as he warns of impending Californian darkness. This is followed by an unaccompanied guitar solo – Donald lets it rip over nothing but the electronic din of the drums, a starkly effective break in texture. A processed chorus of 'Into the darkness' fades into the solo before a variation of the main riff returns along with a crescendo of synths. Another verse/chorus section resumes before the song ends in a deliciously polyrhythmic collision of riffs and chants.

'Feel the Thunder' (Bloom)

The next song feels like a sequel to the previous one. Spooky textures of synths and reverberated organ sneak in before guitar and bass joins in and Eric intones ominously:

Slicing through the night
Three riders came
Perched on American steel
Riders with no name
Even time cannot reveal
Riders with no name

As we understand, this is another biker story. Whether or not one chooses to link it to Pearlman's biker mythology becomes a matter of choice. Both words and music are by Eric, and the story stands on its own legs; A Halloween story about a group of bikers who, after loading up on 'beer and cocaine' drive themselves to death only to end up haunting the highways as ghost riders every 31 October, 'forever doomed to ride'.

The intro is somewhat unusually followed by a vocal-less version of the chorus before the verse takes over. It's got a cool, funky feel to it despite rocking hard, and Joe plays some nifty James Jamerson style basslines underneath, reminding us how eclectic the band could still be. Eric sounds his raunchiest, in keeping with the lyrics about the party-loving bikers. The chorus is anthemic, with what sounds like both Eric, Donald and Joe chipping in on the harmonies.

A couple of minutes into the song comes one of my own favourite '80s Cult moments, as the song launches into a symphonic break of pure gothic doom and gloom. The synthetic pipe organ and the slow, minor key progression makes this sound like something out of The Damned's *Phantasmagoria* album. After some heavy whammy bar action from Donald and another chorus there is another nice break with tight, muted guitars and hard-hitting drums while Eric sings of supernatural tragedy:

And the fates decreed on that night
Their souls must be tried
Now you can hear them every All Hallows Eve
Forever doomed to ride

This section segues elegantly back into the spectral keyboard chords of the song's intro before the song ends with stormy reiterations of the chorus.

'Let Go' (Bloom, Roeser, Ian Hunter)

This would of course not be a post-*Agents* Cult album without its share of musical missteps, and sure enough, here comes a major blunder. 'Let Go', co-penned by Eric and Donald with additional input from Ian Hunter, is a cock-rock singalong of head-scratching banality, even featuring chants of 'B-Ö-C, you can be whatever you want to be'. We are simply going to skip it.

'Dragon Lady' (Roeser, Broadway Blotto)

Marginally better, but no winner, is Donald's throwaway pop tune 'Dragon Lady'. Co-written by Donald and Broadway Blotto of comedy rock band Blotto, it is musically speaking a decent piece of Buck Pop with a breezy sense of melody and a snappy tempo. The lyrics, on the other hand, seem like a real hack job.

> *Dragon Lady takes you by the heart*
> *Dragon Lady takes you by the heart*
> *Try to run but before you start*
> *Dragon Lady's got you by the heart*
> *Dragon Lady takes you by the heart*

No Nobel material here. The best part of the song is the fact that Rick Downey steers clear of his Simmons drums and puts in a fine, up-tempo performance.

'Light Years of Love' (J. Bouchard, Helen Wheels)

The album thankfully ends on a much higher note with Joe's stately ballad 'Light Years of Love'. It's probably one of the most sentimental numbers the band has recorded, with both the wall-to-wall string synths and borderline cheesy chord progressions threading a fine and dangerous line. But Joe saves it both through an intelligent arrangement and an earnest and sensitive vocal performance.

The verses are built around a simple ascending bass figure augmented by processed guitars and synth orchestration while the chorus expands the texture with more synth and what sounds like a guitar through a rotary speaker doubling Joe's vocal lines – a typically clever touch from the thoughtful Joe. The song's high point and in fact the most poignant moment on the album, is a solo performed by Joe on a classical guitar, beautifully played and heartbreakingly melodic. It leaves you wanting more. Donald takes over briefly on electric guitar before the chorus returns, Joe stretching his voice to the limits. The song slowly fades out over the chorus progression, leaving a heart-warming impression after what is otherwise a slightly cold and technical listening experience.

Revölution by Night is a controversial record in the Cult corpus. Coming on the heels of the acclaimed Martin Birch-produced albums it disappointed some fans with its AOR leanings and the cold, polished sound. Seen from a somewhat wider perspective, though, they got some things right. The first Birch collaboration, *Cultösaurus Erectus*, was hard-hitting and effective, but was a bit more straight-ahead hard rock than what the band was usually known for. *Fire of Unknown Origin* addressed that shortcoming by offering up a more eclectic collection of songs and a darker atmosphere. Even so, it still didn't feel entirely like the Cult of old, which was fine – and it was indeed a great album. But to these ears *Revölution by Night* – for all its techno sheen – actually captures the spirit of the old Blue Öyster Cult more successfully, especially in songs like 'Shadow of California' and 'Feel the Thunder', while also taking the full leap into contemporary sounds with 'Shooting Shark' and 'Take Me Away'.

The end of side B is a bit of a let-down after the two strong biker songs, but that is no different from any post-*Agents* album, that all contained some bloopers. My personal take is that *Revölution by Night* is considerably better than its reputation.

One thing to note is that this was also the first studio album without Albert on drums. Rick Downey is a capable drummer, but cut from a very different cloth than Albert. He is more of a meat & potatoes hard rock drummer, and the songs lack the groove and subtle shuffles that Albert would inject. On the other hand he was a hard hitter and especially at home in higher tempos, and helped infuse some extra energy into the rhythm section.

Again, contrary to the impression people have of the band's utter commercial failure in the mid-80s, the album did reasonably well. The two singles, 'Shooting Shark' and 'Take Me Away', reached 16 and 11 respectively in the Billboard Hot Mainstream Rock charts and received a decent amount of airplay both on radio and MTV. And the album cracked the Top 100 both in the US and the UK.

Even critics took rather kindly to the band's new sound. *Rolling Stone's* Errol Somay liked the album while admitting that it was less innovative than the band's earliest albums. 'Combining patented BÖC pop occultism with Donald 'Buck Dharma' Roeser's incendiary guitar solos, songs like 'Feel the Thunder' are heavy-metal bonecrunchers meant to be played while you're breaking the land-speed record on your motorcycle. Air-guitar specialists, on the other hand, will be sent into spasms by the dazzling sonic effects of 'Take Me Away.'' He also went on to praise 'Light Years of Love' and 'Shooting Shark'.

Creem were even more enthusiastic: '…those boys from the sweet underside of the white underbelly, those stalkers of the rock forest, have once again given us leave to grab up the torches of velocity and render a few more cities on flame with rock 'n' roll.'

A final note on the cover art, once again by Greg Scott. This is one of my personal favourites: An empty, futuristic freeway in dystopian blacks and greys with a doom-laden, lightning-rent sky for backdrop, and a mysterious light, maybe an apocalyptic easy rider, racing down the road. One assumes it's the clover-leaf junction mentioned in 'Shadow of California'. The back of the album features some science fiction mash-up of alien machine and Egyptian god while the inner sleeve has a drawing of the Egyptian dog-god Sirius, obviously a nod to the *Imaginos* myth in which the dog star has such a central place.

On balance, *Revölution* was an interesting, colourful record. It lacked the extreme high points of *Fire of Unknown Origin*, but it was slightly better paced. The main detracting factor in my ears is not the material, which I think overall is very good, but the fact that the production lacked that bottom end meat that made the Birch productions so powerful. *Revölution* has a lovely, multifaceted surface sheen, but it suffers in the low-end register, due to the bright production.

Chapter 11: Do you know Jacques Cousteau?
Club Ninja (Columbia, 1985)
Personnel:
Eric Bloom: vocals, guitar
Donald 'Buck Dharma' Roeser: vocals, guitars, keyboards
Joe Bouchard: bass, vocals, guitar
Tommy Zvoncheck: synthesisers, piano, organ
Jimmy Wilcox: background vocals, percussion
Additional musicians:
Thommy Price: drums
Phil Grande: guitars
Kenny Aaronson: bass
David Lucas, Joni Peltz, Dave Immer, Joe Caro: background vocals
Howard Stern: opening to 'When the War Comes'
Produced at Bearsville Studios, New York, Boogie Hotel Studios, New York, Tallysin Studios, New York and Warehouse Studios, New York, 1985 by Sandy Pearlman
Release date: December 1985
Highest chart places: 63 (US)
Running time: 44:26

The aftermath of *Revölution by Night* was a difficult time for the band. While the record did ok, it failed to fully capitalise on the commercial momentum *Fire of Unknown Origin* had started. Columbia was at a bit of a loss to guide the band forward, and within the ranks discontent grew. Touring continued as always in support of *Revölution*, but even this proved rocky. By the end of 1984 Rick Downey left the band. Albert Bouchard was briefly hired for a stint of touring but was soon out again. In the midst of this turbulence there was also the expectation that the band would record a new album, and maybe make good on the promise delivered by 'Burnin' For You'; that the band was more than a two-hit wonder.

To complicate matters, Allen decided that he'd had it with the band. His involvement with recordings had been in gradual decline for years, and with Donald, Aldo Nova and Larry Fast handling most of the keyboards on *Revölution* it's easy to see that Allen felt he had little to contribute going forward.

Replacements for both Albert (again) and Allen were soon found. Jimmy Wilcox was in the band's orbit already, as a member of Rick Derringer's band at the time. Derringer was a good friend of the band. Jimmy was also Willie Wilcox' little brother, and Willie of course played in Utopia, another band with friendly relations to the Cult. Jimmy proved to be a valuable live asset, but even his tenure would be short-lived as we shall see.

As for Allen's successor, Sandy Pearlman picked Tommy Zvoncheck, who had until then played live keys for Aldo Nova and Public Image Ltd as well as recording for The Dream Syndicate. Tommy was already the hired keyboardist for the still-under-construction mastodon *Imaginos*, and Sandy liked his playing enough to offer him up for the band. Tommy was a good musical fit for the band with his considerable knowledge of modern music technology and vast palette of sounds.

It was decided to bring Sandy on board again for the production of the new album. How much of this decision was the band or the label is uncertain. It seems reasonable to assume that both camps thought that bringing Sandy back into the fold would rekindle some of the old magic. Recordings took place throughout 1985 on the East Coast, in Woodstock's Bearsville Studios, the Boogie Hotel and New York's Warehouse. Even David Lucas was hired for some assistant production work, making it almost seem like the olden days. Not that things really were that rosy.

It took about a year to record the album – the majority of time was spent on overdubs and mixing, while the actual backing tracks were recorded in 30 days according to Joe. It was the most expensive BÖC album to that date.

One of the fateful decisions that were made, and that has stained the legacy of *Club Ninja* ever since, was to bring in outside songwriters. It was a typical late '80s move to provide old warhorses like Heart, Aerosmith and our Canadian friends Loverboy with outside writing help in an effort to appeal to younger and broader audiences. It was perhaps also a symptom of major label jitters in the post-revolution days of punk and new wave, not to mention the hairspray revolution in metal. Label bosses no longer trusted '70s rockers to come up with the goods themselves. The blockbuster days of *Rumours* and *Frampton Comes Alive* were gone, and rock was no longer as commercially viable as it used to be. It was the age of Michael Jackson and Madonna, or airbrushed pop metal like Bon Jovi, rather than the rugged, road-weary hordes of longhaired rockers.

'White Flags' (Leggat bros)

And so it came to be that *Club Ninja*, the band's 10th studio album, opened with a song that no Cult member had a hand in writing. Not that it really sounded out of place. 'White Flags' originally appeared on a very interesting 1982 concept album by Ontario proggers Leggat, led by the brothers Hughie and Gordon Leggat. Leggat occupied a particular niche in Canadian music, the quirky junction of pop, prog and hard rock that also included bands like Max Webster and FM. However, Leggat's sole album has remained an obscurity in spite of its many fine qualities.

Covering 'White Flags' (which appeared on the original Leggat album as a 12-minute epic) was an inspired choice, as it is an engaging, rousing and thought-provoking piece of music. The fact that it was cut down to a more radio-friendly length on the album didn't detract from its appeal, especially since Eric gives it a whole new lease of life with his much more focused and forceful vocal presentation than the original.

The opening 20 seconds of the song contain a lot of information about what's going to happen on the album. One thing is Donald's crisp, chorused electric guitar or the up-front rolling bass. But Tommy Zvoncheck makes his presence felt immediately, first opening the ball with a descending sci-fi synth effect, then fading in under the guitar with the sound of a slowly opening envelope on a synth pad, then underlining it all with a thunderous bass pedal synth, and finally a computer-like sound-effect created by a synth's sample & hold function. It becomes clear that we are dealing with a very different keyboardist than Allen. Allen was a fine, fine keyboardist and composer, but he was not a synthesist, not the kind of synth player that would twirl knobs for an eternity to find the right sound. Tommy, on the other hand was just that – a knob-twirler of the first degree who by his own admission brought 14 synthesisers, a piano and a B3 to the sessions. His indelible stamp is all over the album, and no less so than in 'White Flags'.

The song continues to deliver as whirlwind drums enter, with all the bottom-end punch that was lacking from *Revölution by Night*. People can say what they will about *Club Ninja*, and indeed they do, but there's no denying that from a purely sound engineering point of view it is one of the best-sounding BÖC albums, with punch, clarity and space. While Jimmy Wilcox is credited as the band's primary drummer, it was in fact Billy Idol's Thommy Price who played the majority of drums on the album. Thommy was also a hot item due to having played on Patty Smyth's Scandal's Top 10 hit 'The Warrior'. A virtuoso drummer, Thommy brought energy, precision and elegance to the album.

After the stormy intro, the verse enters with a pulsating bass synthesiser and Eric singing in a restrained, slightly raspy tone that fits the music well. The beginning half of the chorus sees him tackling a lower register than we are used to hearing him in, highlighting new aspects of his singing. Lyrically the song is a poetic take on the tribulations of love, maybe not the most Cultish of themes, but the artfulness of the writing still brings it somewhat into the Cult universe.

Hold me close, don't fear my body
The flesh is weak, in need of touching
Your hands are hungry for want of knowing
Your eyes are closed, but still they're showing
Like the white flags of surrender
The war is over, the battle's ended
Like the snowflake in my hand that's melting
Can't you feel my love?

Around the three-minute mark comes a cool little unison run between Hammond organ and what sounds like a synth bass, injecting some of the Leggat brother's prog origins and also letting the Keith Emerson-influenced Tommy Zvoncheck show some of his true colours. Towards the end of the song Eric is joined by some lovely backing vocals from Joan Peltz, also known as Joan or Joni Paladin, a singer Sandy had discovered. He produced her only album, featuring a lot of the *Club Ninja* cast, only to see it shelved by the record company. Hence her appearance on *Club Ninja* is pretty much her only major credit.

'Dancin' in the Ruins' (Larry Gottlieb, Jason Scanlon)
Next up is the album's hit song, 'Dancin' in the Ruins'. Many fans have been surprised to discover that this poptastic number was not in fact written by Donald, but by professional songwriter Larry Gottlieb. Gottlieb has mostly traded in MOR songwriting, penning tunes for The Four Tops, Marie Osmond and The Manhattans. Incidentally he also wrote the theme song for the 1986 charity event Hands Across America, that was sung by one Joe Cerisano whose acquaintance we shall make in the next chapter.

'Dancin' in the Ruins' is a perfect companion piece to both 'The Reaper' and 'Burnin' For You', a breezy yet rocking tune mixing romance with darker, dystopian themes. Just like with the best of Donald's songs there is a delicate mixture of exhilaration and melancholy at work here. Even though the song is immediately accessible, it also rewards deeper listening. If they had to go to outside writers, they could have done no better than this song. Just like 'Burnin'' and 'The Reaper' before it, this song is in the key of C major whose relative A minor lingers close by. All these songs typically revolve around guitar friendly chords like G, E and A minor, that all ring pleasantly with open strings. These similarities make the song seem immediately familiar, almost as if you've heard it before. And yet the song has a freshness to it, courtesy of the new musicians in the band and neat production touches.

'Dancin'' starts with busy drums, synth punctuations, layers of crisp guitar and an organ before the verses take over with a slight reggae feel to the guitar that hits the off beats, not entirely unlike 'Burnin''. Donald's vocals are upfront and treated to a light, fluffy reverb/delay effect so subtle that it is felt more than heard. The melody has that unique amalgamation of upbeat longing that is Donald's trademark, as he sings:

> *Tomorrow soon turns into yesterday*
> *Everything we see just fades away*
> *There's sky and sand where mountains used to be*
> *Time drops by, a second to eternity*
> *It doesn't matter if we turn to dust*
> *Turn and turn and turn we must*
> *I guess I'll see ya dancin' in the ruins tonight*

The poetic fatalism in these lyrics go far beyond your regular pop fare. The reference to (Donald favourites) The Byrds' 'Turn Turn Turn' is also highly appropriate.

While the choruses brim with the usual Buck Dharma harmonies, the verses are augmented by production touches like tight, muted guitar picking and a bubbling Hammond B3 that always brings back memories of the Black & White period. Dancin'' also showcases the extreme tidiness of Sandy's production on this album. Even the busy choruses manage to exude a sense of space through careful stereo panning of the different elements. Donald also breaks out a small arpeggiated guitar riff reminiscent of 'The Reaper' during the chorus.

After the second chorus Tommy offers up a sort of micro-solo with some funky synth sounds, before the third and most poignant verse arrives. Over a lush bed of synths and little else Donald plays some heartbreaking licks drenched in delay effects, before he starts singing. Thommy provides a pulse with rimshots while Donald plays some almost The Edge-like staccato guitar out in the right channel. The combination of this ethereal soundscape and the downright mystical lyrics makes for one of my favourite moments on the record.

Like marble statues all with gold inlaid
In castles built in silence let us play
Even though our skulls ride in our flesh
We can build a maze of tenderness

It is interesting how a writer with no prior connection to the band managed not only to hit the spot musically, but also provided lyrics that seem to tap right into the centre of the bands mystical, melancholy heart.

The song was a minor hit for the band and had a nifty MTV video made for it that picked up on the post-apocalyptic vibe of the lyrics. It was somewhat innovative in that it was a film showing the filming of a mock-documentary about a future skater gang doing their thing in the ruins of civilisation. Very post-modern.

'Make Rock Not War' (Bob Halligan jr.)

The next tune is one of the reasons why *Club Ninja* tends to top everyone's 'worst BÖC album' list. 'Make Rock Not War' is written by Bob Halligan jr, who is not a nobody in the world of rock. He has contributed songs to Judas Priest, Halford, Kiss and even Cher. For AOR aficionados he is especially well-known for having co-written most of the songs on the seminal – and semi-legendary – Icon album *Night of the Crime*. There's no doubt that Halligan is a good writer, and musically I find 'Make Rock Not War' a lot less offensive than previous Cult duds like 'Hungry Boys' or 'Let Go'. Lyrically, though, it falls flat on its face in a BÖC context with its banal anti-war sentiment. For a band that made as spine-chilling a portrait of the suffering soldier as 'Veteran of the Psychic Wars', lyrics like these are an embarrassment:

Tell me, make rock not war! What are we dying for?
Rock not war! Nobody wins!
Rock not war! What are we trying for?

So instead of lingering on the lyrics that no-one can argue are substantial, we'll focus on the music. The song mostly fits within a heavy AOR template, carried by eight-note pulses on bass and guitar, power chords and grandiose bursts of keyboards colouring the sound. The rhythm section here as elsewhere on the album is tight and uncluttered, one of the most praiseworthy aspects of the album. But the one thing that stands out for me, and that saves the song from complete forgetfulness, is Tommy's B3 organ, that swells and ebbs organically and adds life and size to the song. Without that element the song would have been wholly unremarkable.

'Perfect Water' (Roeser, Jim Carroll)
Luckily, we move swiftly from the mediocre to the absolutely sublime. Donald's collaboration with writer/singer Jim Carroll, 'Perfect Water', is a fan favourite, a concert staple and one of Donald's classic Cult compositions. Carroll, famous author of *The Basketball Diaries*, had been in the band's social circuit for some time, having among other things shared an apartment with Patti Smith (whom he dated for a while) and Robert Mapplethorpe. Because of this connection he was closest to Allen Lanier, who both played and contributed songwriting to Jim's albums.

In the year of the album's release, 1986, Jim Carroll taught a poetry class and spoke to his students at length about the song. It gives some interesting insights:

> *It's on the new Blue Öyster Cult album, actually – I always liked the Blue Öyster Cult – I mean, this friend of mine, Allen Lanier, wrote a lot of, well, a couple of, the only ballads I have on my first and third album. (...) I didn't tell them how I wanted, how I heard the music, and it came out so different from the way I heard it, it was interesting to find that out, you know. (...)'*

He goes on to explain that he had also given the lyric to The Doors' Ray Manzarek, who had also written a tune to it.

> *'But the one thing he did was, he didn't get it. I knew there had to be: 'This is perfect water, passing over me' – and the real line I liked was – 'Do you know Jacques Cousteau?/Well, he said on the radio'. You know, it had to be, really, like, casual there, and he had it, like, real slow, the rhymes didn't even hit, you know.*

So, Carroll was fairly satisfied with Donald's interpretation. The words describing aquatic mysteries are perfectly accompanied by scintillating, clean guitar chords, glittering like sunlight on water, while subtle synthesisers evoke the underwater refractions of that light. The clean guitars are heavily compressed to bring out pick attack and to make them sound 'up-close and personal', making for an intimate soundstage. The vocals are crystalline, Donald sounding his absolute purest as he enunciates the poet's words:

> *Perfect water*
> *The dark wind braids the waves*
> *The crazed birds raid the trees*
> *Is this our destiny?*
>
> *To join our hands at sea*
> *And slowly sink*
> *And slowly think*
> *This is perfect water*
> *Passing over me*

To my ears this is one of the most perfect marriages of words and music that the Cult ever committed to tape. The structure of the song is very organic, it's hard to tell where a verse ends and a chorus begins. It flows in a serpentine manner without any clear breaks. A whole half-minute goes by before the drums enter, leaving the beginning of the song in a weightless state. Once the rhythm section enters, the drumming is replete with spacious tam fills and swooshing cymbals, while the kick and snare seem to follow esoteric and less than obvious meters. At times the drumming here reminds me of that master of subtle complexity, Phil Collins. Joe's bass guitar was elected out for 'Perfect Water'. The bottom end is instead provided by another Imaginos sessionist, Kenny Aaronson. As is easy to hear from his nimble and uncluttered playing on this song, Aaronson is a virtuoso on his instrument. He shares a history with Thommy Price in Billy Idol's band, but his credits include anything from Hall & Oates to Bob Dylan. For baroque pop nerds, it is also notable that he played in The Left Banke keyboardist/writer Michael Brown's post-Banke project Stories, who had a no. 1 hit in 1973 with a cover of Hot Chocolate's 'Brother Louie'.

Aaronson and Price's interplay on 'Perfect Water' is in any event a joy to listen to.

As the song unfolds we can hear Sandy and the boys pulling out all the production stops, with lush, layered harmony vocals, bright, bell-like synth sounds to complement the lyrics and of course some searing lead guitar from Donald. 'Perfect Water' is without a doubt the record's musical and lyrical highlight.

'Spy in the House of the Night' (Roeser, Meltzer)
Next up, and rounding off side A, is a cool little tune called 'Spy in the House of the Night'. A co-write between Donald and Meltzer, the lyrics are on the silly side, possibly a paean to stoner-dom.

I have no church or philosophy
I've never known or told a joke can't you see
I smoke in bed
I smoke instead
I know the ins and outs of smoke

And when there's smoke there's fire
The flipside of desire
And if it's true
It can't be you
Might as well be me

Musically this is a fairly rockin' Donald number, in a guitar solo-friendly midtempo. One of the most notable aspects of the song is Tommy's driving Hammond organ, that rolls and bubbles with heavy use of the speed control on the Leslie rotary speaker. It gives a mid-range depth to the song and creates a lot of textural movement. Tommy also embellishes with some rhythmic keyboard elements, like some nicely timed staccato clavinet stabs. I suspect the bass is played again by Aaronson, although this has not been confirmed by anyone. There appears to be some slapping involved, which is not usually within Joe's domain of playing.

Donald adapts a style of singing here that is more in the Tom Petty/Don Henley school of rock'n'roll than his usual sensitive style, more in the vein of how he sang on his solo album *Flat Out*. His guitar solos on 'Spy' lean more towards the blues than on the rest of the album. My only regret is that Tommy doesn't get a shot at a Hammond solo here – it would have fitted perfectly.

'Beat 'Em Up' (Bob Halligan jr.)

Side B starts on a low point with another Halligan song, 'Beat 'Em Up'. On the one hand this is an almost ridiculously simplistic pop metal sing-along bordering on the parodic. The lyrics are not even worth quoting. Musically it's not particularly interesting either. What it does have going for it is again Tommy's lively keyboard work, especially the Hammond, as well as a forceful if not exactly soulful vocal performance from Eric. It is also in some ways a precursor to the up-tempo metal, albeit of the more serious kind, that the band would explore post-*Imaginos*.

'When the War Comes' (J. Bouchard, Pearlman)

Things improve vastly on the epic 'When the War Comes', the only Pearlman lyric on the album. Music courtesy of Joe, this is a doomy, dirge-like number that seems like a perfect follow-up to *Revölution*'s Pearlman contribution, 'Shadow of California'. Like any Joe song, it moves through myriad chord changes and an unusual structure. It also does not feature a standard lead vocal, the verses are instead mostly harmony vocals led by Joe. Like 'Perfect

Water', 'When the War Comes' also has no discernible separation into verse-pre-chorus-chorus, but rather comes off as one, long, continuously shifting melody in keeping with Joe's prog rock-influenced writing. The sound here is incredibly dense and layered, with multiple guitars and keyboards intertwining atop cavernous drums. In fact, this song is quite close in production style to the controlled chaos unleashed on *Imaginos*. A recurring and remarkable texture in the song is a bright tubular bell sound from Tommy's synth that somehow cuts through the din. Says Tommy, 'That sound was several DX7's midied together using the tubular bells sound', a testament to his prowess as a synthesist.

Lyrically this song is definitely part of Pearlman's occult rock'n'roll revolution narrative:

A vision
All hail the revolution
Armies of the past retreat
In the wake of revolution
A journey to the country
Of the fourth dimension
Spectacle of awakening light
The soldiers are baffled but still they fight

There are also interesting references to both Hinduism (Shiva, the god of creation and destruction) and the New Testament (Matthew 10:34: 'Do not think that I have come to bring peace to the earth. I have not come to bring peace, but a sword.'):

Creator, destroyer, victory, defeat
I did not come to bring us sleep
Black flag, red flag, space and time
The future is my mind

The fact that Sandy replaces the biblical 'peace' with 'sleep' is in keeping with his Gnostic take on Judeo-Christian myth, since the Gnostics equated the spiritual status quo of the world with a 'sleep' from which the spiritually curious must awake to gain true insight (*gnosis*). It stands to reason that any agent of Pearlman's revolution would come to awaken his followers, rather than support that status quo. The revolutionary/millenarianist strain in Gnosticism can be found throughout Pearlman's writings for the band.

The outro to 'When the War Comes' is noteworthy. We are left alone with Tommy's DX7 bells and Thommy Price beating frantically at his toms, interspersed with pinched harmonics from Donald's guitar, creating a stark, almost avant-garde soundscape before the song ends. Famously, the spoken word intro to the song was recorded by radio personality Howard Stern, who was a friend of the band.

'Shadow Warrior' (Bloom, Roeser, Eric Von Lustbader)

The music for 'Shadow Warrior' had originally been written by Eric and Donald for submission to the 1984 comedy *Teachers* but was never used there. Eric, being the pulp culture connoisseur that he is, instead came up with the idea of commissioning a lyric from writer Eric Van Lustbader, known for his string of ninja novels that helped popularize the genre in the West. 'There was a guy, Eric Van Lustbader, who wrote a book called *The Ninja*, which I loved, so I reached out to him to write some Ninja lyrics for ('Shadow Warrior').' (Interview *i94bar.com*)

Von Lustbader came out of vaguely the same culturally thriving '60s/'70s East Coast cauldron as the Cult boys, having grown up in Greenwich Village, a neighbour of Lauren Bacall and a childhood friend of actor brothers Keith and David Carradine. He started out as a music writer and is credited with having opened the door to the American market for Elton John. In later years he has among other things found success as a writer for the *Jason Bourne* series of books that was started by Robert Ludlum.

A ninja theme seemed like a natural progression after the band's declaration of love for Japanese pop culture with 'Godzilla'. Lustbader's lyrics fit in surprisingly well in the Cult's swelling corpus of literary lyrics, this one reflecting previous themes of cosmic fates and lonely warriors.

I have no home
I live within my mind
I have no one
No one
I bring the earth and the sky with me

Her face, the image of a thousand stars
A bridge between tomorrow and today
If we destroy one another
Dawn will never break the day

'Shadow Warrior' is the most successful of the heavier, up-tempo tunes on the album, with an infectious main riff and a grandiose melody. The rhythm section is keeping it very basic here, allowing the chunky guitars and Hammond organ to occupy most of the space. A bridge section is particularly glorious, with soaring organ and power chords and Eric singing passionately about a 'Spirit singing/A song of the ages', before the drums kick into double-time and Donald blows through a speed metal-like solo section. This is a rare instance where the band captured a particular aspect of their live shows – the double-time instrumental blow-out – on album, and it is worth the price of admission alone. The song returns first to the gothic bridge melody, ending with a heavy metal scream from Eric before some verses and chorus and finally a return to the speed metal guitar solo. 'Shadow Warrior' is an exhilarating ride and a damning argument against those who claim *Club Ninja* is low in energy. Live the song came particularly alive, as witnessed on the much bootlegged 1986 Santa Monica concert.

'Madness to the Method' (Roeser, Dick Trismen)

The final song on the album is a lengthy piece by Donald called 'Madness to the Method'. It's a slow, majestic tune with a Pink Floyd vibe to it, in part thanks to the almost painfully slow tempo. It starts off with drums that are again reminiscent of Phil Collins, with a gated reverb that increases their size and impact. On top of this comes an arpeggiated guitar figure and some dramatic piano. The sound of the intro is expansive. Things are stripped down as the verse arrives atop a simple, slow drum beat, languid piano chords and interesting, rhythmic synth punctuations. Donald's vocal melody is also sparse, but emotionally laden.

Lyrically the song seems to deal with the teenage wasteland of macho rivalries and mating rituals.

It's a hormone war zone
The boys are out for a fight
Wenches in the trenches
On a Saturday night
Stick it here, stick it there
Get it out of sight
It's the time and the season
For the nasty things at night

Throughout the song Tommy's synths and piano provide dimension and colour, and in the whole the song has been very carefully and successfully orchestrated. Tommy proclaims it his favourite track on the album: 'It's kind of fusion'.

At seven and a half minutes it does not seem too long. The guitar solo moves into decidedly Gilmour-esque territory with long, arching blues lines, but also some speedier runs. At the end of the song we are treated to a wonderful, classically-infused piano solo from Tommy, a rare moment on the album when he is allowed in the spotlight. An original ending to an album that, while heavily flawed at times, features some genuine highlights and thanks to both the rhythm section and the strong keyboard presence shows the band in a new, fresh light.

No-one is going to argue that *Club Ninja* is the greatest BÖC album, or even in the Top 5. But just like other controversial albums by the band it needs to be understood as a product of its time, and of the situation the band was in. The outside writers came in due to a lack of confidence in the band on the part of the label. Not the best move, but in 'White Flags' and 'Dancin' in the Ruins' they still managed to score a couple of effective songs. 'Dancin'' was a popular song on MTV, got modest airplay and placed no. 9 on the Billboard Hot Mainstream chart. The album peaked at 63 on the Billboard 200, which was of course a disappointment considering the time and money spent on the album, but at least they were still in the charts.

As for the original material on the album, things were far from as dire as some writers would have it. 'Perfect Water' was a bona fide classic, while tracks like 'Shadow Warrior' and 'When the War Comes' took the darkest, heaviest aspects of *Revölution by Night* and matched them with a production more sympathetic to the material. As I have touched upon, Sandy's meaty production of the album also pre-shadowed the gargantuan soundscape the world would hear once *Imaginos* was let loose on the world.

Credit must also go to Tommy Zvoncheck's invaluable contributions to the album. Commenting on how he got involved, Tommy says: 'Sandy asked me to 'ghost play' on the album'. Of course, he soon became the band's official keyboard player. He found the recording experience a mixed bag. 'Cutting basic tracks were fun. Overdubs were long, gruelling sessions.', although he is careful to point out that 'Donald was very helpful'. When I asked him about his wide array of synths used on the record, he had the answer ready. 'Memory Moog, OB8, Prophet 5, DX7, TX-816 rack, Korg EX-800, Mini-moog, Oberheim Matrix 12. Hammond C3, acoustic piano. Maybe some Wurlitzer.'. As for his prog influenced style, 'I absorbed stuff from all the great players of the '70s. I think my love for the Doors was what endeared me to the BÖC guys.'

Retrospective reviews of *Club Ninja* tend to pan it. *AllMusic*'s William Ruhlmann notes that Sandy Pearlman's re-entry into the group's orbit 'did nothing to arrest BÖC's decline into musical anonymity.' And the website Ultimate Classic Rock has the album coming in last in their 'best to worst' ranking of BÖC albums.

However, contemporaneous reviews were more open to the updated sound. Metal magazine *Kerrang!* concluded that 'The masters of highly polished platinum Metal return after a two-year absence with their best work since *Cultösaurus Erectus*', while *Sounds* were appreciative of Sandy's production and called the album 'a seemingly leaden slab of AOR which suddenly turns into gold in your hands'.

While the album did little to assuage Columbia's fears that the band's commercial capital was dwindling, it was still not enough of a failure to keep the label from making one last, monumental bet on the band, as we shall see in the next chapter.

Chapter 12: Dance a Don Pedro
Imaginos (Columbia, 1988)
Personnel:
Eric Bloom: vocals
Albert Bouchard: guitar, percussion, vocals, associate producer
Joe Bouchard: keyboards, backing vocals
Allen Lanier: keyboards
Donald 'Buck Dharma' Roeser: guitars, vocals
Additional musicians:
Tommy Morrongiello, Jack Rigg, Phil Grande: guitars
Tommy Zvoncheck: keyboards
Kenny Aaronson: bass
Thommy Price: drums
Joey Cerisano: vocals
Jon Rogers: vocals
Jack Secret: additional vocals on track 2
Shocking U: backing vocals on track 3
Daniel Levitin: guitar sounds (uncredited)
'Guitar Orchestra of the State of Imaginos':
Marc Biedermann (lead guitar on track 1)
Kevin Carlson
Robby Krieger (lead guitar on tracks 7 and 8)
Tommy Morrongiello
Aldo Nova
Jack Rigg
Joe Satriani (lead guitar on track 5)
Produced at Kingdom Sound Studios, New York, Boogie Hotel Studios, New York and Alpha & Omega Studios, California between 1981 and 1988 by Sandy Pearlman and Albert Bouchard
Release date: July 1988
Highest chart places: 122 (US)
Running time: 55:01

In 1915, one Isaac Newton Phelps published an immense book named *The Iconography of Manhattan Island*, 1498-1909, with a subtitle reading 'Compiled from original sources and illustrated by photo-intaglio reproductions of important maps, plans, views, and documents in public and private collections'. I have not read the whole thing, and I don't know if anyone has. It's a mélange of war history, spiritual history, geography and all manner of things relating to Manhattan and surrounding areas. But there is a curious reference to Long Island there. Quoting from a private letter, Phelps writes: 'the place of destination is a secret, but Long Island or New York are generally talked of as the place of rendevous (sic) . . .'

Then, in the mid 1960s, bookworm, philosopher, student and Long Island inhabitant Sandy Pearlman writes a poem, or collection of poems, called *The Soft Doctrines of Immaginos*. This is the only part of the original poem known to the public:

> *My destination is a secret*
> *And the doctrine is soft*
> *And just between the verse and me*
> *It's a place where you can see*
> *Lost, last and luminous*
> *Scored to sky yet never found*
> *Relics of jewels*
> *And ant-track tools*
> *A true ghost dance*
> *Rehearsal Ground*

Pearlman probably never read Phelp's strange book, but there is a pleasant symmetry here, since Pearlman was known to be very interested in the history of his own home turf. For one thing, his neighbourhood was H. P. Lovecraft's old stomping ground, and Brown University, where some say Pearlman studied, although no record of this has been found, was Lovecraft's model for Miskatonic University, home of terrible, forbidden books.

Brown University's real history is no less strange. Located in Providence in Long Island's neighbouring Rhode Island, its John Hay Library actually contains rare examples of anthropodermic bibliopegy, the art of binding books in human skin. If that weren't enough, the place was also infamous for the fascist leanings of some its alumni in the 1930s. One of the students was the infamous White Russian fascist Anastasy 'Annie' Vonsiatsky, who legend has it would drive to the school in a large convertible dressed in full Nazi regalia. This image is of course reminiscent of both the BÖC song 'Boorman the Chauffeur' and the cover of 'On Your Feet or On Your Knees', so it seems likely the Nazi-fascinated Pearlman knew of these stories. Brown University was one of many ingredients in the story of *Imaginos*. In a 1975 *NME* interview he explained the genesis of the Imaginos myth:

> *It's about a child who grew up in New Hampshire and discovers he has the ability to reconcile the imagined with reality. There's no gap between his imagination and his ability to realize it. He can accomplish what he imagines and imagine what he's going to accomplish. Secret Treaties began the concept with the Desdinova theme. The new thing is called 'The Soft Doctrines Of Imaginos'. See, I like to use naive, densely stupid terms. It's a trick of some Russia literature to totally obliterate metaphors. Anyway, Desdinova is a student at Brown University in Providence who lives there to be close to Lovecraft. He's a Frankenstein figure who*

achieves through research what Imaginos understood instinctively, he forms the axiom. Desdinova appears in 'Astronomy' and some of the songs yet to come out.

To fully understand the historical and geographical context of the Imaginos myth, we must understand the soil from which it sprang, the ground on which its creator walked, which is why I thought the opening quote from *Iconography* was appropriate. Long Island, Rhode Island, Connecticut – what we generally know as New England, is indeed a 'secret destination' for those interested in the occult and esoteric. In the very beginning, New England was the realm of the free-thinkers, the people who had fled persecution for heterodoxy in the old England. The result was a culture ripe with heretical Christianity and old European folk beliefs that eventually mixed with some Native American lore as well. It is not without reason that the persecution of 'witches' started here. And it is this cauldron of weirdness that Lovecraft pours from in most of his stories. In his paper *Vampires and Death in New England*, author Michael E. Bell describes the 'occult New England' well, contrasting it from the more chaste, Calvinist 'mainstream New England':

> *The other New England, radiating from outlying towns in Rhode Island and eastern Connecticut, occupied geographic and philosophical margins. It extended up the Connecticut River Valley into Vermont and New Hampshire, reaching into southern Maine. This territory, surrounding the Puritan lands, includes precisely those areas where a supernatural worldview coexisted with Protestant ideology and, not coincidentally, where the vampire tradition has been documented. The residents of these areas were, in John Brooke's words, 'close spiritual kin to the sectarians of revolutionary England' who rejected any connection between church and state, advanced doctrines of a miraculous restitution of the true church and state, advocated free will and universal salvation, and at its extreme announced a perfectionist ideal of human divinity. As the work of John Edward Christopher Hill, Keith Vivian Thomas, and many others have amply demonstrated, the sectarian theologies of the Radical Reformation and the radical wing of English Revolution accommodated and perpetuated what we classify as magical or occult beliefs.*

It is in this New England that the seeds were sown for what literary historian and author Harold Bloom calls 'the American Gnosis', a tradition that Sandy Pearlman places himself firmly within with his cosmology of New England heresy, alchemy, aliens, Kabballah, Egyptian mysticism and Native American magic. *Imaginos* is above all a modern Gnostic myth.

But it doesn't end with the ancient and arcane. A relatively modern occultist, Aleister Crowley, spent periods between 1916 and 1918 in New Hampshire, birthplace of our hero Imaginos. Crowley was interested in a site called Mystery Hill, a place of archaeological interest sometimes called the 'American Stonehenge'. Lovecraft reportedly made a trip to the same area, that inspired both *The Dunwich Horror* and *Whisperer in Darkness*. While in New Hampshire, Crowley mostly stayed in a cottage in Hebron, just at the foot of Cannon Mountain, where America's first and arguably most famous alien abduction allegedly took place. On September 19th, 1961, Barney and Betty Hill claimed to have been abducted by aliens from the Zeta Reticuli star system after first having spotted a UFO near Cannon Mountain.

A bit further south from New Hampshire, and a bit later, in the 1970s, the enigmatic Process Church set up headquarters in Massachusetts. Famous for their rumoured involvement in the Charles Manson murder case in California, the Process Church had an image that was more sinister than their actual teachings, a sort of New Age Christianity. But with their swastika-like logo, their propensity to recruit biker gangs for protection and their habit of walking around with leashed Alsatians (a German shepherd-like dog) while wearing black, it is easy to see both how they may have frightened East Coasters – and fascinated Pearlman. Many see the German shepherds (or are they Alsatians?) on the cover of *Secret Treaties* as a reference to the Process Church and their falsely rumoured practice of ritually killing the dogs, while the idea of biker gangs protecting a group of spiritual revolutionaries is of course right out of Pearlman's apocalyptic biker universe – as is the combination of occultism and Nazi symbolism. Add to this that the East Coast chapter of the Process Church also got linked with our old friend, serial killer Son of Sam, as well as Patti Smith and Allen Lanier's roommate, photographer Robert Mapplethorpe, and you see where it is all going.

So, it is no wonder that a young Sandy Pearlman's head was filled with thoughts of wonder when he sat down, surrounded by the ghosts of New England, to write his *Soft Doctrine of Imaginos*.

An extremely condensed reader's digest of the story goes thus: In the heartland of occult weirdness, New Hampshire in the early 19th century, a 'modified child' is born. Imaginos knows no boundaries between his imagination and the real world. What he imagines, becomes real. Wanderlust takes him far and wide. After a journey to Mexico he is shipwrecked. Mysterious entities, Les Invisibles (the Loa of voodoo, or aliens, probably both) approach him with an offer: Drown in the Gulf of Mexico or be resurrected to his true destiny. Reborn as Desdinova, master of shapeshifting and intrigue, he wears many disguises through history, changing history according to his will (or according to the Invisibles' will?). As a British sea captain, he revisits Mexico to discover a black mirror, sister mirror to Elizabethan magician John Dee's magic mirror, inside a Mayan pyramid, in a jade chamber of impossible angles (very Lovecraftian). He brings it out of the jungle 'by crime' and home to his granddaughter in Cornwall. That mirror is in fact an organism ('an organism-beam riddling voices direct to the brains of the (European) multitudes'), spreading a disease of darkness in Europe until the two World Wars break out.

In other words, a very convoluted story about the occult origins of Europe's World Wars.

We have already gleaned that the *Imaginos* concept was something the band was working vaguely with from the beginning. But because the band eventually wanted to free themselves from Pearlman's influence, an actual concept album never saw fruition. So in 1981, Albert and Sandy decided to work on the album apart from the band. The long gestation time of the album is the stuff of legends, and the story is complicated. Eric Bloom broke it down to manageable size in a *Musicradar* interview:

> *Imaginos is like the Blue Öyster Cult album that isn't a Blue Öyster Cult album. It was kind of an Alan Parsons Project-type thing that Sandy worked on with Albert – this was after Albert was let go from the band in 1981. It's really a concept album the two of them did. The label didn't want to put it out for a while, but it was eventually issued as a BÖC record.*
> *I wrote the song called 'Subhuman' in the band house in Eatons Neck. It was on the Secret Treaties album. Originally, it was called 'Blue Öyster Cult', but we couldn't call it that because it was the name of the band. It reappears as 'Blue Öyster Cult' on Imaginos. The album was Sandy's long, epic poetry that he wrote in the '60s. He and Albert did it with studio musicians. It took three years and hundreds of thousands of dollars for it to finally be finished, and then Columbia didn't want to put it out. It sat on the shelf.*
> *Finally, it was put to us that the label would put it out if it was called a Blue Öyster Cult record and if Donald and I sang the material. Buck and I went into the studio, we played and sang, and that's how it ended up what it is. On one hand, it sounds like a BÖC record, but on the other hand, it's kind of a left-field record. For a concept record, it works. It's definitely different.*

It was predominantly Albert's vocal that rubbed Columbia the wrong way. They didn't feel it was strong enough to carry the whole album. Also, after all the money they spent on it, they felt it was safer to release it as something the public would recognise – a BÖC album, rather than the less-than-household-names of Albert and Sandy. The final recordings featuring the other members of the band, predominantly Eric and Donald, were done in Sandy's studio in San Francisco. I remember reading an interview with Sandy and the boys at the time, possibly in *Kerrang!*, where everything seemed rosy – they were talking about driving out to the Golden Gate bridge in the twilight after a day's session to listen to rough mixes and see if the vibe was right.

Now, for the music. It was decided to sequence the album differently from the actual sequence of the story, hence the description on the album: '*IMAGINOS*: A RANDOM ACCESS MYTH'.

'I Am the One You Warned Me Of' (A. Bouchard, Roeser, Pearlman)

The first track, 'I Am the One You Warned Me Of', is actually the story of Imaginos after his shipwreck, when he has become Desdinova, a wordplay on the new destiny of which our hero has become aware.

The song starts with a heavily compressed and reverberated drum intro before the central riff enters. It's a simple riff made massive by multiple guitar overdubs and expansive reverb. The sound is dense, and the bass guitar has been given a liberal dose of treble to cut through the busy mix. First-time listeners were probably a little shocked by the production, as especially this opening track veers closer to actual heavy metal than anything the band had previously done – quite surprising after the synth-heavy previous two albums. The beat is heavy and sturdy, courtesy of Thommy Price, *Club Ninja*'s virtuoso drummer. It is worth noting that while *Imaginos* to a large extent is Albert Bouchard's album, Albert does not in fact play drums here. Thommy is the main drummer, with Albert adding percussion from time to time, but on *Imaginos*, Albert is primarily composer and rhythm guitarist.

Eric takes the vocal lead here, as on much of the album, and sounds fantastic. Gone is the slight reticence of the previous two albums. He gives a full-bodied, gruff performance that recalls the menace of *Secret Treaties*. The vocals have been recorded and mixed to convey the full range of his timbre, with a lot of depth. Underneath vocals and guitars is a faintly-mixed Hammond, played by Tommy Zvoncheck. A lot of rhythmic interest is created by added guitar parts that provide muted 8ths or other subdivisions, something that was less common on older BÖC albums but is in keeping with '80s production philosophies and the arrival of guitar players like Andy Summers and The Edge.

The title of the song is a bit deceptive as it makes it sound like some sort of a bad boy anthem, but the lyrics are anything but heavy metal clichés. Sandy reaches the apex of his poetic powers on this album, and the depth of cryptic allusions is boundless. Probably only Pearlman himself could decipher it all for us, but unfortunately it's too late for that.

Fresh from zones of moisture
And afterwards the meat
With spangles on my long-tailed suits
And songs to haunt the one that's saved

Just call me Desdinova
I'm sure to be
The lucky one
When destiny assigns wisdom
Known to me
The starry wisdom

We understand that 'fresh from zones of moisture' refers to Imaginos' near-drowning in the Gulf of Mexico, and that he is 'the one that's saved'. 'Destiny assigns wisdom', through his saviours Les Invisibles, and that wisdom is the 'starry wisdom' that Pearlman borrowed from H. P. Lovecraft's universe and that is referred to in the liner notes of *Secret Treaties* as the 'secret science from the stars. Astronomy.' In Gnostic terms we could say that this is the song about Imaginos after his spiritual awakening, and that Les Invisibles are the agents and messengers of that *gnosis*, that spark of starry wisdom. It is also worth noting that a drowning in water is an alchemical symbol of transformation. In alchemy one is not reborn to spiritual purity before one has undergone a death of sorts in water, the alchemical *solutio* in which the old order of things dissolves. A well-known alchemical image is that of the 'drowning king', which C. G. Jung interpreted as the death of the ego, the immature mind, a necessary prelude to rebirth and purification. Sandy was well-versed in alchemy and certainly knew this when he let his hero drown, only to be reborn with a new name and purpose.

The song ends with a hyper-active lead guitar which may be one of the many session guitarists rather than Donald, as it doesn't sound like his trademark licks. Underneath, Thommy Price holds down a Bonhamesque, stomping beat, ending the song on as heavy a note as it began.

Many fans are sceptical of the final released version of *Imaginos* because they feel the original Sandy/Albert versions of the songs were 'purer'. But compare this to the version on the 'demo *Imaginos*' that is floating around the internet, and you realise that what happened was for the best. Eric's voice elevates this song to classic BÖC status and brings out all the mystery and magic of Pearlman's lyrics.

'Les Invisibles' (A. Bouchard, Pearlman)

Our next randomly accessed chapter is *Les Invisibles*. This is in fact the beginning of the story according to Sandy's original sequencing. The entities Les Invisibles, once we start deciphering the story, appear to be somewhat like Lovecraft's Great Old Ones, godlike creatures of extraterrestrial origin. The song's lyrics place their origin, not surprisingly, in the constellation of Ursa Major, and through other *Imaginos* lyrics we can identify the star of origin as Sirius, the brightest star in the night sky. The lyrics cleverly mix allusions to astronomy and extraterrestrials with voodoo symbolism, which is underscored by the use of the term 'les invisibles', which is borrowed from voodoo religion and is an alternative name for the *Loa*, the spirit creatures. The *Loa* are known to have separate personalities and are identified with individual dances, music and moods, something Sandy references in the song.

Dance a Don Pedro
Do the Don Pedro
Games after death

Night dances 'round
Samedi and Petre
In Alchemy

Don Pedro is a popular *Loa*, protector of Haitian farmers and thus a guardian of fertility, while *Petre*, or *Petro*, is a class of fiery *Loa* characterized by the colour red. Samedi is one of the Baron Loas, belonging to the *Ghede* class of *Loas* characterized by the colour black. The reference to alchemy thus makes doubly sense in that Sandy's obsession with the Red and the Black can be traced back to the alchemical process of transformation, where black (*nigredo*) is the beginning stage and red (*rubedo*) is the final, purified stage. Clearly the bottom line here is that Sandy equates the *Loa* with his Invisibles from outer space, and alchemy is the special science brought from the stars. And the song 'Les Invisibles' is our introduction to these entities, who instigate the whole narrative.

Musically 'Les Invisibles' is a clear highlight on the album. It opens with a synthesiser pulse doubled with a muted, staccato guitar. The guitar then breaks out in the occasional chord to define the progression before humungous drums and a bass join in. It's a hi-tech, mysterious sound unlike most of what we have heard before from the band, except maybe some of the more Tommy Zvoncheck-dominated moments on *Club Ninja*. And Tommy's touch is all over this record, and especially in this song. Says Tommy: 'Allen played on the basic tracks for a day or 2. I remember because I had a gig that weekend I couldn't get out of. Tom Mandel was also on the basic tracks and did some overdubs. I ended up replacing *all* the keyboard parts for various different reasons. As parts are added some parts don't work as well as the track develops.' So in the end it is Tommy's synthesisers and keyboards we hear on the album.

Donald then takes the vocal lead with a sinuous melody, and again the vocal production is noteworthy. Donald's voice sounds full and present, and the processing applied is subtly tucked behind the actual voice so as not to reduce clarity and intelligibility. A deep choir of 'seven-seven-seven...' intrudes periodically to add a touch of mystery to the proceedings. During the verses the song lingers over an A drone represented both by the synth pulse and by Kenny Aaronsen's deftly played bass that dances around the root note. The strong anchor of the root A and the insistent rhythmic pulse of bass guitar and synth creates a hypnotic atmosphere very much in keeping with the lyric's descriptions of magical dances and cosmic pulses ('the rhyme of the star clock'). There is a starkness to the harmonic underpinnings of the song, with few but effective chord changes. The chorus moves the song up to a D, while a guitar break moves into Donald's favourite oscillation between A, G and F. A second chorus-like section also overlays these chords, and features typical airy Buck harmonies. Throughout the song Donald's voice is occasionally treated to a reverse reverb that adds to the spacey, mysterious atmosphere. The lead guitar through the entire song is definitely Donald himself, and he ends the song on a frantic, semi-chaotic note reminiscent of song endings on *Tyranny and Mutation.* All in all, 'Les Invisibles' is one of the most unique and effective songs on the album, with its mixture of hi-tech sounds and occult strangeness.

'In the Presence of Another World' (J. Bouchard, Pearlman)

The next track, 'In the Presence of Another World', is both one of the most musically pleasing on the album, bordering on progressive rock, and one of the most lyrically obtuse. The most likely reading of this song is that it deals with Imaginos/Desdinova's time in England, where he studies Elizabethan magic as laid out by famous magician and royal counsellor Dr. John Dee. As the liner notes tell us, it was here Imaginos heard of John Dee's 'obsidian mirror' and its magic powers. Dee was also known to dabble in the kind of magic that opens doors to the spirit world. The lyrics speak of 'a bridge of paper/Inscribed with a hundred names of God'. This bridge is the bridge to another world. In the Jewish mysticism of the Kabbalah, which Dee was well-versed in, the names of God were a gate-opener. Thirteenth-century Kabbalist Joseph Gikatilla, for instance, thought the secret names of God unlocked sacred dimensions to the practitioners of Kabbalah.

So Imaginos uses Elizabethan magic and the Kaballah to open a door and stand 'in the presence of another world', one that seems quite terrifying.

In the presence of another world
A dreadful knowledge comes
How even space can modulate
And earthly things be done

This is perhaps when Imaginos becomes fully aware of the awesome and terrifying, world-changing power that he wields. The end of the song appears to question the moral wholesomeness of whoever is pulling the strings in this cosmic drama. Is it a Gnostic demiurge – an arrogant, meddling demi-god who likes to wreak havoc on worlds, or perhaps one of Lovecraft's evil gods, dwelling in a buried city in the stars. Maybe they are one and the same, as many have pointed out similarities between Lovecraft's Old Ones and the demiurges of Gnosticism. In any regard, it is clear that it is this entity that leads Imaginos to the piece of perfect black that will bring chaos and war to the world.

Your master is a monster
And gentlemanly too
He'll make for us some new germ
With pieces of the perfect black
The alpha and omega
The double peaks of Mars
The maze of his infinity
The buried city
In the stars

'In the Presence' was written during the band's earlier days, by Joe, and was kicked around during sessions for a few of their albums without ever quite making the cut. Perhaps it was 'too much Sandy' for the rest of the band. In any event, it is one of Joe's finest and most ambitious compositions. It opens with a very characteristic chord, fingerpicked on a clean guitar – the E minor add9. This is the very same chord that opened the title track of the album that came to instigate and define progressive rock – King Crimson's *In the Court of the Crimson King*. It is the self-same album from which brother Albert borrowed some of the riffs in 'Cities on Flame'. It is a moody, somewhat unstable chord that has found favour both with prog rockers and heavy rockers. It forms the basis of Metallica's 1986 'ballad' 'Welcome Home (Sanatorium)', and it also features heavily in the ending instrumental 'Sunset' on German prog rockers Eloy's 1980 album *Colours*. Indeed, the similarities between 'Sunset' and the intro to 'In the Presence' are more than a little striking, and later in the song some soft, glissando lead synth also recalls Eloy.

The opening chord establishes a floating, and indeed otherworldly atmosphere that is further enhanced by ethereal piano twinkles and pillowy synth sounds.

The 'quiet' first section of the song is sung by Jon Rogers, who for a short time was Joe's replacement in the band after Joe's departure. He is the bass player on the 1986 *King Biscuit* radio broadcast from Santa Monica which in this author's opinion is one of the band's finest live recordings. His voice is like a cross between Donald's and Eric's, full-bodied and powerful yet soft and sensual, and fits the quiet, elegiac melody to a tee. Jon would incidentally also go on to play and sing in Donald's short-lived project The Red and the Black, whose posthumously released album features an early version of 'Harvest Moon', a song we will hear about later.

After about a minute and a half the drums enter with full force, and a prog metallic ascending riff takes over. Eric arrives on the stage, invoking Sandy's Frankenstein-like imagery – 'your master is a monster'. A choir section then takes over, repeating the monster warning, before a shredalicous guitar solo arrives, backed by full, heavy riffage. The solo ends abruptly, and Eric comes back in with a dramatic melody atop Supertramp-like synthesized piano and tense unison lines on bass and guitar. Everything calms down, the pastoral opening chords return before things slowly build to an incredibly sinister crescendo with chugging guitars, blazing drums and the remaining lyrics whispered/spoken/sneered by a female voice credited to one Shocking U, apocryphally rumoured to be Patti Smith. The whole song is an immense demonstration of the dynamic and stylistic range of the 'band' at this point, and while it could easily be called over-produced, there's no denying the efficacy of Pearlman's Wagneresque vision here.

'Del Rio's Song' (A. Bouchard, Pearlman)

Before digging into 'Del Rio's Song', which in the original sequence of events fits in between the songs 'Imaginos' and 'Blue Öyster Cult', let's get a little background. The historical backdrop of Sandy's story stretched way beyond Imaginos' birth in the early 19th century. It is the Spaniard's discovery of the New World that is the real genesis. Or rather, anti-genesis, in Sandy's words: 'To the Spaniards, the first Europeans to find a New World, what they found was not good. It was anti-genesis, anti-Eden, seat of evil, pit of darkness.' He goes on to say that all of Mexico's golden metal was no 'luminous mirror of delight' but a 'mirror of blackness'. The New World was, he says, 'in the thrall of invisible spirits', and the gold, symbol of the alchemist's penultimate goal, inspired the worst instincts in people, 'striven for beyond all limits'. The gold of the New World gave the Spaniards power, but that power quickly corrupted those who wielded it. It was, as the story bears out, the same Promethean power that dr. Frankenstein wielded – limitless, beyond morals, potentially evil.

So, this is the background for Imaginos the adventurer's perilous trip from New Orleans in 1829 towards Mexico. The lyrics seem to suggest that a vision ('eyes that glow') inspired the journey:

So packed with eyes
That glow like coals
And pointing towards the North
Oh my boat left New Orleans in 1829!

As for the music, 'Del Rio's Song' is one of the most classic, Cult-sounding songs on the album. It's fairly simple, opening with thundering power chords and pounding drums that lead into the chorus. The Hammond organ swells underneath the layered guitars while the bass pushes steady 8th notes amid a sea of drum reverb. It's audacious, over-the-top and quite deliciously rock'n'roll! Eric sounds the best here that he has done in about 20 years, delivering with all his force and with perfect control of his vibrato. Around the two-and-a-half minute mark a funky little hard rock riff takes over before a barnstorming guitar solo erupts over ever more frantic drumming. Things are then taken down quite a few notches as a pivotal moment arrives, the recital of the only known actual poetry from *The Soft Doctrines*, the one I quoted at the beginning of this chapter. The words are delivered in a frantic whisper, processed with a flanger effect and echo. It's a moment of heightened tension, a sense of suspended time. The listener is made to feel like the entire album spins around this one, central moment. The voice rises in pitch and intensity towards an orgasmic crescendo of wordless voices and bent guitar notes before the chorus returns again. Of all the songs on the album, this is the one that most faithfully recaptures the magic of the band's hard-rocking glory days.

'The Siege and Investiture of Baron Von Frankenstein's Castle at Weisseria' (A. Bouchard, Pearlman)

Side A ends on the most monumental note in the band's entire history. The ridiculously titled 'The Siege and Investiture of Baron Von Frankenstein's

Castle at Weisseria' is at least as gothic as it sounds, maybe a little more. To these ears it sounds like Sandy stepped out of the studio for a day and left the keys to Jim Steinman. It is the very definition of *Sturm & Drang*.

In Sandy's original sequencing, this song comes after 'I Am the One You Warned Me Of', and as Sandy writes in the liner notes, it is a tale of 'the new destiny unleashed'. Desdinova is now fully aware of his powers, godlike, Promethean, an American Frankenstein. And indeed Sandy places him 'in the heart of the American Rhineland', which in the overlapping universes of the Imaginos mythos is simultaneously the occult landscape of New Hampshire and the no less mythic landscape of the German Rhineland. It was here, by the town of Darmstadt, that Mary Shelley found the Frankenstein castle that allegedly inspired her famous story about the mad doctor and his monster. The actual Frankenstein castle was inhabited in the 1600s by the alchemist Johann Conrad Dippel, who it was said invented an elixir of life, Dippel's Oil. Whoever imbibed it would become immortal. Dippel was also rumoured to conduct hideous experiments on corpses he exhumed, and it was indeed whispered that with the help of the power of lightning he brought the dead back to life. So, with this in mind we understand that Desdinova was indeed a dr. Frankenstein, one who held the key to life and death, world without end. This song doesn't really have too much bearing on the actual progression of the plot, but can be seen more as a meditation on Desdinova's powers.

It could be argued that 'The Siege' is the heaviest song BÖC ever recorded. It starts off with a thunder-squall and then three measures of a slow, doomy drum beat that is the closest the band ever got to Black Sabbath. A semi-chromatic descending sequence of foreboding synth notes start spinning atop the drums before the guitars finally kick in. The atmosphere set by the intro puts you right in some gothic castle scene out of a Hammer horror movie, which was probably Albert and Sandy's intention. The guitar riff is very much in the Tony Iommi vein, monolithic, simple and sinister. Hearing the song out of context, one could be forgiven for thinking this was a late '80s doom metal act. And still, there are more surprises. As the vocals enter, listeners are forgiven for feeling a few moments of confusion. Indeed, here is an intense heavy metal singer of immense force, just like Eric Bloom – except it's clearly not Eric Bloom. 'The Siege' is sung by Joe Cerisano. An immensely talented singer, Joe had his own band in the early '80s, the AOR-inflected Silver Condor, but he is better known to larger audiences through his many commercial jingle stints for brands like Coca-Cola, General Electric and Miller Beer. He has also sung back-up with Michael Bolton and more recently has been one of the singers with symphonic metallers The Trans-Siberian Orchestra. As mentioned in the *Club Ninja* chapter, he also sang on 'Dancin' In the Ruins' composer Larry Gottlieb's Hands Across America theme song. Whether that had something to do with his appearance on *Imaginos* is unknown. Either way, if Sandy and Albert insisted on an outside singer for 'The Siege', they couldn't have found a better fit. Joe's performance on the song is one of the album's highlights, melodramatic and theatrical and in several senses of the word, pitch perfect.

Even though the basic riffs of the song are relatively simple, there are layers and layers of sound here. The song employs female backing vocals to great effect, subtly underneath Joe's vocals and more overtly towards the end of the song. Tommy Zvoncheck's keys are pushed to the background, but no less effective, with baroque piano flourishes and soaring synths. Thommy Price's drums are the backbone, and his performance is outstanding, combining Zep-like swagger with his own precise, hard-hitting style. Around the two-minute mark there is a break in the groove as a lead guitar enters, first tentatively with some pinched harmonics and restrained licks before the band kicks in again and the full force of Joe Satriani's formidable talent is unleashed. The solo is a piece of music in itself, with complex runs, mind-melting acrobatics and unmatched intensity. Joe Satriani's work on *Imaginos* actually facilitated the making of his seminal solo album *Surfing with the Alien*, since he traded his guitar playing on *Imaginos* for free studio time for his own album. Joe's playing here is another album highlight.

The second half of the song almost defies description, as it turns into a strange mixture of church music and gothic metal, with a beautiful, ethereal chorus of 'world without end' blending with aching, funereal guitar lines from Buck and heavily reverberated drums. For a while, as the drums fall away, one is tricked into thinking the song has ended, before the chorale and the multitracked guitar melodies enter for a final encore. 'The Siege and Investiture of Baron Von Frankenstein's Castle at Weisseria' is a strange, heady, heavy journey that honours the band's earliest ambitions of mixing Black Sabbath with psychedelia, and it is perhaps best summed up by this line from the lyrics:

A drug by the name of World without end

'Astronomy' (A. Bouchard, J. Bouchard, Pearlman)

'Astronomy' follows this blow-out. The 1974 ballad got redressed for *Imaginos*. Because it was completed at an earlier time than the rest of the material, its lyrical tone is a bit different. It bears less overtly on the actual narrative and is more peripherally Imagin-esque. We've already delved into the lyrics when dealing with the *Secret Treaties* version, so we'll skip to the music. In *Agents of Fortune*, Albert tells Martin Popoff that he was thinking about 'Edge of Seventeen' when they arranged the tune for *Imaginos*. Sure enough, over a pad of choir-like synth the chugging 8th-note staccato guitar from that Stevie Nicks song turns up. It establishes a much stronger rhythmic feel for the song and gives it a forward motion that the original lacks, for all its simple elegance. The *Imaginos* 'Astronomy' is less timeless but more immediate, and it is quite beautifully sung by Donald.

As the drums gradually increase in volume through the first verse, the second verse arrives with upfront drums and a very funky bassline from Kenny

Aaronson. I remember being a bit taken aback the first time I heard this. I thought it was a little disrespectful to turn a sombre ballad into a funky pop song. But over time I've learned to like it, and the lighter, bouncy feel adds new life to the song.

The song develops throughout, with the pre-chorus spiced with some gang-chanted 'hey, hey-hey's. Counteracting the staccato and funky feel of the song is Donald's interpretation of the melody: He lingers longer on the notes and brings out the mellifluous nature of the vocal lines even more than the 1974 version. The second half of the song is mostly taken up by some jammy guitar over the basic rhythm and progression, before the 'Astronomy, a star' section closes things out.

Columbia were hopeful that Donald's smooth vocals and the familiarity of the song might propel it into the airwaves or the charts and released it as a single. There was also a promo video made for the British market with a spoken word intro by Stephen King.

'Magna of Illusion' (A. Bouchard, Roeser, Pearlman)

Things are kicked up a notch or three with what would on any other album be called the magnum opus, except that *Imaginos* is a whole series of magnum opuses – or is that opi? 'Magna of Illusion' is one of the most complex and fully realised tracks on the album – strictly speaking a progressive rock track with added crunch.

The track opens with crushing power chords and more of Tommy Zvoncheck's trademark pathos-filled piano, before a muted electric guitar establishes a weighty trot over which Donald takes the lead vocal. It is rare that Donald gets to show his more theatrical side within the BÖC context, but here he gets to use his full expressive range, relating a tumultuous tale of Desdinova as he secures the black mirror in Mexico and brings it back on a perilous journey, to finally deliver it to his granddaughter in Cornwall.

Stories on land, storms at sea
'Tween 1892 and '93
When Granddad sailed for Mexico

'Magna of Illusion' is a wordy song, with Sandy in his ultimate storytelling mode. There's descriptions of Cornwall, a sort of British equivalent to New Hampshire with its pagan and mystical traditions ('where witches went mad more than once') and there's detailed accounts of the perilous journey to Mexico ('And when the sun proved false/As it always does/Some of them would be lost/And some would sail back home'), and then the return to England and to the granddaughter. But what could have been a tedious exercise in words is instead a compelling musical journey. The vocal melody is unpredictable, with long lines dictated by the lyrics rather than traditional rock meter, and swells of Hammond organ, tremulous synths and baroque flourishes of piano punctuate proceedings in sync with the story being told. The long melodic lines also require long harmonic progressions, which is one of the things that places the song more in a prog rock tradition than a hard rock one. In some ways the song has more in common with the old '70s Genesis epics than with anything coming out of the hard rock scene in the '80s. Instead of short riffs we get long chord sequences that develop in an almost orchestral manner.

After about four minutes of melodic, lyrical and harmonic complexities, a further high point arrives with a spoken word section. It is August 1 (remember those Dog Days), exactly one year after Desdinova left for Mexico. He returns, with his dangerous gift:

> *That night the Captain's granddaughter*
> *Would celebrate her birthday*
> *'I've come a long way,' said the Captain,*
> *'From Lost Christabel this night.*
> *Accompanied by my dog familiar,*
> *To blast your rafters with my surprise.*
> *Granddaughter, it's a foreign mirror*
> *Taken from the jungle by crime!'*

I was seventeen at the time when the album came out. I bought it on the day it was available in the stores. And when I listened to it for the first time, this part made me laugh out loud with elated satisfaction. It was exactly the kind of pleasing creepiness that a teenager raised on horror movies and hard rock was born to appreciate. An innocent girl receives a gift from her cosy grandfather, a gift so poisonous and dangerous that it will start two world wars ... Satisfyingly dark.

Desdinova's last message to his granddaughter is both illuminating and foreboding:

> *Behind closed eyes*
> *Realise your sight*
> *Mine, granddaughter, proves a surprise*
> *More light than sun,*
> *more dark than night, then*
> *More a snare than lust*

'Blue Öyster Cult' (Bloom, Pearlman)

The song ends with a dying squall of feedback and a tortured synth note, and then arrives another redressed 1974 nugget. The track 'Blue Öyster Cult' is actually Eric and Sandy's old tune 'Subhuman', but this time heavily musically rearranged. In the original sequence of events, Blue Öyster Cult/Subhuman follows 'Del Rio's Song', and tells of Imaginos' alchemical near-drowning and subsequent rescue at the hands of Les Invisibles/the Blue Öyster Cult.

The lyrics have been rearranged, and much has been added. Specifically, there are more overt references to the alchemical/mystical rebirth:

> *Recall the dream of Luxor*
> *How fluids will arrive*
> *As if by call or schedule*
> *Resume through the morning tide*
> *Where entry is by seaweed gate*
> *And plan the plan of dreams*
> *To lose oneself in reverb*
> *In all that is and all that seems*

This new reference to the 'dream of Luxor' is significant. Luxor, on the banks of the Nile, was a place of worship and of mystical significance. To the old Egyptians the river Nile was sacred, and its annual inundation and the flooding of surrounding plains were a symbol of rebirth. The waters of the Nile were both literally (for crops) and symbolically life-giving, and the temples of Luxor were filled with rituals of rebirth, especially associated with the god Osiris, whose own story of death and rebirth closely resembles the alchemical narrative of transformation.

So Imaginos/Desdinova is now placed within that context, the miraculous reviving of the drowned wonder boy took place in waters that symbolically were the life-giving waters of the Egyptians and the alchemists.

All this mystical tale-spinning must of course be matched by the music, and indeed the song starts off with some rather cosmic-sounding synths, again reminiscent of proggers Eloy. As the verse starts, a folksy-sounding clean guitar takes over and Albert, for the first time on the album, grabs the mic for some lovely lead vocals. Things are kicked up with a more rhythmic chorus of sorts, backed by a catchy guitar riff and harmonies from Donald. There is also another spoken word part here, and the vocals are processed to sound ethereal and mysterious, with some more of that backwards reverb we've heard before on the album. 'Blue Öyster Cult' is not the most musically successful song on the album. It starts out nicely with the atmospheric synths, the warm guitar and Albert's very humane voice. But it is over-long, almost seven and a half minutes, and the second half of the song seems to disintegrate and loose direction with meandering guitar and the incessant chanting of 'we understand'.

'Imaginos' (A. Bouchard, Pearlman)

'Imaginos', the final track on the album, is an interesting one. It would probably place in the beginning of Sandy's original sequence, seeing as it deals with Imaginos' arrival in the world and his early years.

> *Imaginos*
> *Approached the sun*
> *In August in New Hampshire*

> *Singing songs*
> *Nobody knew*
> *And stories left undone*

We've already covered the ground in terms of his birthplace and birth month. The song goes on to cryptically allude to an early life filled with wild adventures and changing identities.

> *I'm Buzzardo in Texas*
> *I'm a pinwheel in Vermont*
> *And gorge the Bungo Pony*
> *I'm a rocker a roller and a spinner, too*
> *Below that scene of subterfuge*
> *Which is*
> *On the border*
> *The last exit to Texas*

Texas appears to be his last adventure before he heads to New Orleans and attempts his first journey to Mexico.

The song starts off with a funky riff featuring saxophones (uncredited in the liner notes). The funky feel, the horns and the Stax-like rhythm guitars make it feel like a song that could have been written by Allen Lanier, but it is in fact another Albert tune. Kenny Aaronson gives it his best here, with some very infectious bass lines, while Tommy Zvoncheck cooks it up with rocking piano and burbling Hammond. Musically it's one of the most uplifting and energetic songs on the album. Some listeners could probably do without the 'oooh, Imaginos' chants, just like they could the similar chanting in the previous song, but by now we've come to expect some degree of silliness from the Cult. The song is well arranged, with dynamic ebbs and flows. Jon Rogers, who we heard on the album's first track, takes the sole lead vocal here, but mostly one doesn't reflect on the fact that it's not one of the Öyster boys themselves doing the singing. Towards the end the song turns into a bit of a soulful funk jam, with guitars and saxophones interweaving over the tight backing before the song ends abruptly. It's an unusual and uncharacteristic ending to a Cult album, but maybe that's exactly what makes it quintessentially Cult.

Your opinion of *Imaginos* will be colored by your opinion of Sandy's role in the band and the significance of the Imaginos story. If you feel that the BÖC is primarily the actual boys in the band, and that individual songs trump any overarching concept, you may think that *Imaginos* is an overblown piece of indulgence and deceit. And that is a valid enough point. *Imaginos* IS overproduced, and probably a bit overcooked. But if, on the other hand, you see Sandy's myth-making as essential to the band, and if you have been looking for clues to Imaginos ever since *Secret Treaties*, then *Imaginos* the album is a treat. It is where the story comes together, and it is where Sandy's lyrical universe gets to shine fully, without the intrusions of non-related music and lyrics. From that perspective it matters less that it started out as an Albert solo album, and that Donald and Eric were merely flown in for a few sessions to make it a Cult album. Because a Cult album about Imaginos is as Cult as it can be.

I can appreciate both points of view, but I primarily subscribe to the latter. It is fantastic to get the whole story told, albeit in jumbled order, from beginning to end, and the music matches the words gloriously. *Imaginos* combines the progressive hard rock of *Tyranny* and *Secret Treaties* with the heaviness of the Birch era records and the high tech sheen of *Revölution* and *Club Ninja*. Is it too processed, too heavy on the reverb? Yes, but I am not sure that this album could have worked if the production wasn't over the top.

In that respect it compares neatly with another hard rock concept album that came out the year after *Imaginos*, Jim Steinman's *Pandora's Box*. That is also an album steeped, if not drowned, in gothic melodrama, and in heavy-handed production techniques and spoken-word interludes. And it shares *Imaginos*' semi-ridiculous conceptual frame-work, albeit not the mystical aspects. But both albums are consistent in their tight-rope balancing act between the powerful and the ridiculous – and both albums in the end pull it off.

Inevitably, the public did not see it in quite the same way. Columbia were dumbfounded as to how to market the album, and Sandy and Albert had spent so much money on the recording that there was probably nothing left for promotion. So, the album was pretty much left to sink or swim. And naturally, a proggy concept album about aliens and alchemy did not swim particularly well in 1988, a year of hair metal and dance pop. Two singles were released, one with 'Astronomy', which reached no. 12 on the Billboard Hot Mainstream Rock Tracks but never reached the actual singles chart. The other single was 'In the Presence of Another World', which did not chart at all. The album itself peaked at #122 in the Billboard Hot 200 but ended up selling only 50 000 copies in the US, an immense disappointment for the label.

Critically, however, the album fared better. *Rolling Stone's* David Fricke deemed the album their best since *Secret Treaties*, which is the highest praise the band could get. He went on to explain that while it is not quite properly a BÖC album, 'even in this altered state, it is vintage heavy Öyster menace, a nightmare mosaic of brooding Gothic chorales, flame-thrower riffing and snappy crackling pop. 'I Am the One You Warned Me Of' commences the protagonist's career of evil with a full anthemic dose of vocal *Sturm* and guitar *Drang*; 'In the Presence of Another World' alternates between Stygian balladry and epic ensemble rage, with background vocals that sound like the Transylvanian Tabernacle Choir.'

The striking cover art is part and parcel of the *Imaginos* experience. It's a dramatic black and white photograph of the Cliff House, a landmark in San Francisco. It burnt down in 1907, but before that the Victorian chateau perched on a cliff housed a popular restaurant. The image is a turn-of-the-century photograph with a suitably apocalyptic and stormy sky in the background.

Sandy had originally planned on getting Greg Scott to do the cover art, and Scott did start the work, but in the end the label decided something more photographic and less fantasy-like was appropriate, which turned out to be a good decision.

The aftermath of *Imaginos* goes a little bit beyond the scope of this book. Suffice it to say that it did not end well for the band's 'reunion'. Albert and Sandy had a falling out over production credits that ended in legal troubles, and Donald and Eric, who had never strictly speaking been a proper part of the project, silently snuck away to make other plans.

Chapter 13: A change in the weather
Heaven Forbid (CMC, 1998)
Personnel:
Eric Bloom: guitars, keyboards, lead vocals on tracks 1, 3, 5, and 7,
Donald 'Buck Dharma' Roeser: guitars, keyboards, lead vocals on tracks 2, 4, 6, 8-11
Allen Lanier: guitars, keyboards
Danny Miranda: bass guitar on tracks 1, 4-9, 11, backing vocals
Jon Rogers: bass guitar on tracks 2, 3 and 10, backing vocals
Chuck Bürgi: drums on tracks 1-8 and 10, backing vocals
Bobby Rondinelli: drums on track 9
Additional musicians::
George Cintron: additional vocals
Tony Perrino: additional keyboards
Produced at Millbrook Sound Studios, New York by Buck Dharma, Eric Bloom, Steve Schenck
Release date: March 1998
Running time: 41:17

Nothing much was heard from the band for a long, long time after *Imaginos*. The band did go out on a short tour to support the album, playing a couple of songs from the actual album, but mostly golden oldies. After that the band transitioned into their 'on tour forever' mode, playing clubs, fairs and biker events and building a reputation as a fun, energetic legacy act.

At that point I didn't expect anything new from the band, until in the mid-'90s a friend of mine sent me a strange CD he had found in LA. It was a soundtrack to a B-movie called *Bad Channels*. The cover blurb claimed that it was a soundtrack by Blue Öyster Cult. The truth was that it was two BÖC songs, some instrumental padding from Donald's home studio, and some forgettable heavy metal songs from forgettable heavy metal acts. The interesting thing was those two songs, because they were, in fact, brand new. It turned out the band had started a collaboration with cyberpunk author John Shirley, and out of that, two songs had come – 'Demon's Kiss' and 'The Horsemen Arrive'. They were no-nonsense, hard-rocking songs with zero frills. 'Demon's Kiss' was an up-tempo vampire song, while 'The Horsemen Arrive' was a doomy exposition of some evil conspiracy. I got mildly excited, especially when news came shortly afterwards that an actual album was in the making, tentatively called *Ezekiel's Wheel*.

When the day finally arrived, in 1998, the album title had changed to *Heaven Forbid*. Many things had changed. They were no longer on Columbia. Instead they had been picked up by CMC, a label that specialized in reviving '70s and '80s hard rock and arena groups in their twilight years. That usually meant setting them up in smaller studios on smaller budgets and focusing the marketing on a smaller target audience rather than having lofty ambitions of chart-climbing and nationwide airplay. CMC have been widely criticised for some less than stellar 'comeback' albums, but in BÖC's case the concept seemed to work well.

Even the band was new. Since *Imaginos*, Eric, Donald and Allen had toured with several different bass guitarists and drummers. When the time came to record *Heaven Forbid*, they had more or less landed on bassist Danny Miranda and drummer Chuck Bürgi. Miranda is a fellow Long Islander whose resume to date includes live stints with Queen and sessions for Meat Loaf. His impeccable technique and powerful tone are all over this album. Chuck Bürgi happens to be one of this author's favourite drummers. Who else could successfully step in for Phil Collins in fiery fusioneers Brand X? Bürgi was also the drummer in the phenomenal AOR project Balance, with Bob Kulick. A true virtuoso, his CV is a who's who of rock, from Billy Joel to Diana Ross to Rainbow. So needless to say, if there were shortcomings on the comeback album, they would not come from the rhythm section. The first tracks that were recorded for the album featured our old pal Jon Rogers on bass instead of Miranda.

The band did the main bulk of recording and mixing in Millbrook Sound Studios, New York, under the watchful eye of veteran engineer Paul Orofino. His no-nonsense approach to recording and mixing really benefits the album, as the sound is shockingly clear and full. Many low-budget comeback albums in the 90s suffered from poor production values, but that was not the case here. Paul got to the core of the BÖC sound, cut out the extraneous and distilled a powerful, hard-hitting audio experience.

'See You In Black' (Bloom, Roeser, John Shirley)

The ball opens with a thunderous drum fill and high-octane blues licks, before 'See You in Black' settles into its thrash metal-like riffage. It was not what anyone expected, I think, when they put on this CD back in '98. Listeners were becoming accustomed to reunited '70s groups putting out mellow, low energy records at this time, just so they could have something to sell at gigs. Instead, BÖC sounded more energetic than – well, ever, really. This was pure heavy metal and ironically, the band that inspired Metallica took their cues from their own students. Scooped, thick guitar sounds chugging away at breakneck tempos filled the soundstage as 'See You in Black' assaulted listeners, and when Eric comes in on vocals, he is sounding re-energised too. He practically screams John Shirley's clever lyrics about a guy who covets his neighbour's wife and fantasizes that her husband is dead.

The wind plucks your black lace gown
You're standin' proudly beside his grave
I see you wearing black
Gently smiling and oh so brave

The drum sound is in your face, with Chuck Bürgi employing double bass drums for that pounding thrash sound. Pretty early on Donald comes in with an adrenalized guitar solo that shows that he spent his time since *Imaginos* practicing and honing his skills. The two post-*Imaginos* albums could easily be said to be BÖC's 'guitar albums', where Donald shines more brightly than ever.

The song wastes no time, and after little more than three minutes the exhilarating ride is over, without the listener quite knowing what hit her.

'Harvest Moon' (Roeser)

Things get a lot more familiar on the next tune, a tune that was known to many fans as it had been a live staple for a few years. Donald's lovely 'Harvest Moon' picks up the reins directly from '(Don't Fear) The Reaper', with a creepy, atmospheric lyric, pretty, arpeggiated guitar figures and gorgeous vocal melodies.

It opens with those spacious guitar chords, before Bürgi picks an interesting beat, marking every downbeat on the snare drum, and Donald switches to a funkier, Steve Cropper-style rhythm guitar. The lyrics, when they come in, are intriguing and well-written, reading like a condensed Stephen King short story. The stage is set with an idyllic, almost Steinbeck-like landscape, maybe California ('the Spaniards settled here'), but then you sense a shadow, with references to war that 'took the best from here' and farmers losing their livestock and moving south instead. Hard winters and mysterious happenings threaten the peaceful veneer. And then there's the disappearances:

> *I sense the darkness clearer*
> *I feel a presence here*
> *A change in the weather*
> *I feel some evil here*
> *I hear some frightful noises*
> *I don't go out at night*
> *Since Bobrow's youngest daughter*
> *Disappeared from sight*

Donald's lyrics retain the best from the band's literary legacy, at once romantic, intriguing and chilling, a perfect companion to 'The Reaper''s lyrics.

A little past the two-minute mark there is a surprise in the form of an abrupt change into double-time with Donald delivering a guitar solo that borders on speed metal. Not what you'd expect from an otherwise lush mid-tempo pop song, but somehow it works well, especially given the dark subject matter of the song. The solo is tripartite, with Donald employing three different sounds and slightly different styles. It ends with a harmony run down the scales before the opening chords return again and the last verses and chorus follow.

'Harvest Moon' is clearly a song Donald cares about, since he also recorded it with is The Red and the Black project, and it is a constant staple in the live shows. And indeed, it is a late career high that rubs shoulders with 'The Reaper', a remarkable achievement.

'Power Underneath Despair' (Bloom, Roeser, Shirley)

'Power Underneath Despair' returns to the more metallic sound of the opening track, but at a more moderate tempo, and steeped in atmosphere. A captivating tale of revenge, it tells the story of a man who ends up in jail after having been framed for a crime someone else committed. He breaks out and finds the man responsible for putting him in jail. John Shirley's lyrics describe well how the power to exact revenge has built up during his desperate time in jail.

> *In solitary for two steel years*
> *Thought of you sixty times an hour*
> *Fighting madness and fighting despair*
> *Digging the hidden power*

The fact that Eric's voice had grown a bit gruff by 1998 only adds to the sense of harsh desperation, and the song is among many vocal highlights for Eric. The song is also a good example of how well the no-frills approach to production works here. The main focus remains on the guitars, with especially the power chords in the verses filling things out without other things getting in the way. It's an anti-*Imaginos* approach, understandably, and it works. The only overdubs to speak of are the dense vocal harmonies in parts of the song. The chorus is a bit of clever musicianship, as the first half is in 8/8 while the second is in 7/8, and Chuck 'turns' the drumbeat around for that second half in a confusing and entertaining way.

'X-Ray Eyes' (Roeser, Shirley)

'X-Ray Eyes' is a fun dip into the guys' past, as I am sure '60s sci-fi flicks were something they all enjoyed. Shirley's lyrics reference the 1963 movie 'The Man With the X-Ray Eyes', with old-school actor Ray Milland as the tragic protagonist.

The music is classic pop-Cult, with a sound reminiscent of the best parts of *Mirrors*. The song opens with a crisp, strummed acoustic guitar before Donald's choir boy voice enters. The verses are augmented by a theremin-like synthesiser from Allen, a clear nod to '50s/'60s science fiction soundtracks. Even though the song is mellow, Donald still manages to squeeze in some cool quickfire riffage, and the song is given extra propulsion by busy bass playing from Danny Miranda.

Some of the lyrics can – probably unintentionally – be seen as a criticism of *Imaginos* – both the hubris of the album and of the character himself. Where *Imaginos* sought to lift the veil on all mysteries, and pierce them with his 'glowing eyes' – 'behind closed eyes, realise your sight', Shirley warns in his lyrics:

Do not envy who sees beyond the pale
Don't look there, pluck not at nature's veil
Do not envy the man with the x-ray eyes

Judging by what happened to Ray Milland in the movie (he blinded himself), it's probably sound advice.

'Hammer Back' (Bloom, Roeser, Shirley)

'Hammer Back' follows, and returns us to a mildly thrashy landscape, with a tight little metal riff forming the backbone. The lyrics seem to be a comment on gun politics, warning to keep the 'hammer back' at all times lest you want to eat someone else's lead.

There's a slight promise of oriental scales hidden within the riffs. And sure enough, after a cool little break of multi-layered melody guitars not a million miles removed from the mellower moments of early Metallica, Donald kicks in with a wonderful solo with both gypsy and oriental inflections, like a metal caravan through the desert. Bürgi's relentless drumming must also be commended on this track, keeping the energy at maximum throughout.

'Damaged' (Roeser, Shirley)

Next up is a rather serious song, 'Damaged'. It starts with a blues riff that sounds like it's coming through a telephone, while Donald does a spoken word intro that is darkly introspective:

Wish I was a better person
With more control
Turn the other cheek
When the punch comes, roll
Wish I was a kinder person
Could see the other's pain
Not overreact, never judge
Shrug off the spreadin' stain

It's a catchy tune that is definitely heavy but steers well clear of metal. There's a swampy, Southern tinge to the groove, and a lot of blues in the guitar. The song also benefits from some amazing Hammond playing from guest player Tony Perroni, who delivers a brief but rousing solo a little past halfway through the song. Donald and Danny Miranda are totally in the pocket here, and the song has a wonderful swing. It's also fun to hear Donald really rocking out with his vocal performance here.

'Cold Grey Light of Dawn' (Bloom, Roeser, Shirley)

A personal favourite on the album is 'Cold Grey Light of Dawn'. A drum roll introduces the song before a deep pedal note on the bass, a D, provides anchorage for a slow progression of distorted guitar chords, joined by a subtle synth pad and overlaid with Donald's most emotive lead guitar on the album. The slow tempo, the sombre atmosphere, the deep bass and the long, aching guitar tones all bring Pink Floyd to mind. If the Floyd were a hard rock band, I imagine they could have written this song.

The subject matter is no less sombre. Shirley writes about sins that cannot be hidden from the light of day, be they crimes or adultery. Whatever you did, it will come out in the end:

No matter what you did
No matter who you are
In the fading light
From a middle-aged star
You've seen every blemish
Every sign of age
And it's useless to whine
And it's useless to rage

Shirley shows his true literary powers here with a lyric that is both poetic and deeply mature.

The song is no less so, and along with 'Harvest Moon' it is the one song on this album that truly reaches the artistic heights of the band's classic albums. Eric sounds convincingly distraught and desperate here, and the guitar is simply astounding, one of Donald's all-time performances, with heart-breaking blue notes and thrilling double stops. The rhythm section stays wisely out of the way, providing the same discrete but solid backing that Mason and Waters did back in the day. The song is also augmented by some clever, low-register harmony vocals.

'Real World' (Roeser, Shirley)

Heaven Forbid would have been a stronger album if one or two songs had been left out. One of them is Donald's 'Real World'. Not a bad song by any stretch, but the blues pop ditty doesn't really bring anything new to the table, and doesn't match the pop genius of 'Harvest Moon', or the emotional depths of its following song, 'Live For Me'.

It starts out with cheerful, up-tempo strummed guitar and is followed by a crisp rhythm section that gives the whole thing a Dave Matthews Band vibe. Melodically it's pretty standard fare, and the lyrics, while dealing with an apt enough subject, fall short of the profundity they seem to invite.

We think our lives are real
Amusement parks, our business deals
Stranger still our empty lives
TV replacing kids and wife

Strange Lives consumed with soapy talk
Lives lived in fear of taking a walk

I imagine it's a song that would work well live, since it's fun and fast, but on the album it pales next to its stronger neighbours.

'Live For Me' (Roeser, Shirley)

All is forgotten and forgiven, however, with the arrival of 'Live For Me'. Possibly Shirley's strongest lyric on the album, this song about a man who loses his brother in a car crash, and about their strong, possibly supernatural bond, is matched to perfect music by Donald. It starts with a haunting electric guitar melody over a mid-tempo groove. The verses are simple in their arrangement, with a muted guitar doubling the 8th notes from the bass guitar and rhythm guitar providing harmonic context. Donald employs some unusual and pretty guitar voicings here, using 2nds to great effect.

His voice has that gut-wrenching vulnerability as he delivers Shirley's words.

It was a wet night
And the other guy
Was lubricated with a pint of Jack
His truck hit
Jimmy's Chevy
With a sound like a thunder crack

I was working late but I felt it happen
I knew that my brother was laid low
I waited for the call
And then the damn call came
And I knew what I knew and didn't want to know

It's the kind of songwriting that puts you right in the moment, and everything in the song furthers the feeling of loss, but also the hopeful message from the brother beyond the grave:

Live for me
Live twice as big
Love twice as long
Work twice as hard
Play all of your cards
Live for me
Live for me
Burn twice as bright
Three times as long
But brother, don't do no one wrong

The song features no production hocus pocus, just a great progression, a stirring melody and class A lyrics.

'Still Burnin'' (Roeser, Jon Rogers)

'Still Burnin'' was presented as a sort of follow-up to 'Burnin' For You', but musically it has nothing to do with that song. It's an interesting tune in that it is one of very few Blue Öyster Cult songs that shows a very clear influence from another band – in this case Missouri art rockers Kings X. 'Still Burnin'' could almost be an outtake from Kings X' classic *Gretchen Goes to Nebraska* album. Both the hard rock funk, the semi-jazzy guitar chords played with a slight crunch, the close vocal harmonies and Donald's melodic profile here are clearly paying tribute to Kings X. It is not a total surprise, since in 1988, following the *Imaginos* release, the Cult toured with Kings X and the two bands got along quite nicely.

It's a cool, elegant rocker that sounds unlike anything else on the album, but it injects a good energy to the proceedings and is a good showcase for Donald's guitar.

'In Thee' (Lanier)

The album ends on a very mellow note with an unplugged live rendition of 'In Thee'. It's hard to see a real justification for including a live version of an old song on an album that is already over-long, but my guess is that they wanted to show the fans what they could expect to see if they went to one of their shows. It's a pleasant enough version, but such an intense album had deserved a more energetic ending.

More than anything, *Heaven Forbid* was a huge surprise. That the old boys could rock so hard, and come up with such captivating material, was not something most people expected – especially after the exhausting experience of making *Imaginos*. It seems that both Eric and Donald built up a lot of steam both as performers and songwriters during the gap years, and that all came out on this record. Another key to the album's artistic success is lyricist John Shirley, whom William Gibson has called 'the godfather of cyberpunk'. Shirley, himself a musician, had been a fan of the band since the '70s.

Says Shirley: 'I happened to be in NYC around 1972-ish, visiting from the west coast, when I went to a free concert in Central Park. Various bands played but the only one I can remember is the Blue Öyster Cult. Their first album was just out or just coming out. They made my eyes snap open wide - they sounded like no one else. That guitar player - there was a sinister liquidity and tonality and a classical intricacy in his sound.'

Coincidences then led him into direct contact with the band two decades later.

'In the 90s mutual friends heard the BÖC were looking for lyricists, and the band was a bit aware of me so I was contacted and began to write for them, starting with a couple of songs for *Bad Channels*, a B-movie I've never seen.

The songs were 'Demon's Kiss', and 'The Horsemen Arrive'. This was a sort of bridge for my getting to participate in the albums *Heaven Forbid* and *Curse of the Hidden Mirror*. I was thrilled to hear Donald and Eric singing my lyrics, and thrilled to hear Allen composing and playing keyboards on songs using my lyrics. I felt like some circuit had closed, completing a mysterious energy flow in my life.' The conjunction of Shirley and the band created a sort of alchemy, not of the Sandy kind, but an earthier, grittier symbiosis that went perfect with the band's heavier sound.

Heaven Forbid did not chart. This was not a shock to anyone involved, since the world had moved on since the '80s, and the airwaves were dominated by post-grunge and 'nu metal'. It did, however, sell enough to please the guys at CMC and to inspire them to invest in a second album.

Critics liked the album too. A contemporaneous review in *The Daily Vault* opens: 'Blue Öyster Cult could be the comeback story of the year', and goes on to praise the tightness of the band and the heaviness of the songs. Germany's important *Rock Hard* magazine loved the album, with the reviewer ending by saying 'I had never expected this band to return with such a strong album. Respect!' Allmusic's retrospective review is a bit more reserved, stating that 'While the band sounds surprisingly muscular and powerful throughout *Heaven Forbid*, the material is below par, lacking memorable hooks or melodies.'

It would be unreasonable to expect the band to match the musical inventiveness of *Secret Treaties* or *Agents of Fortune*, or the grandeur of *Imaginos*, but in sum, *Heaven Forbid* was a pleasing, reassuring and timely return for the band.

Chapter 14: Are you in the pocket of the moment?
Curse of the Hidden Mirror (CMC, 2001)
Personnel:
Eric Bloom: vocals (2, 3, 5, 6, 8, 10, 11), stun guitars, associate producer
Donald 'Buck Dharma' Roeser: lead guitars, vocals (1, 4, 7, 9), producer
Allen Lanier: rhythm guitars, keyboards, background vocals
Danny Miranda: bass, background vocals
Bobby Rondinelli: drums, percussion
Additional musicians:
Norman DelTufo: percussion
George Cintron: background vocals
Produced at Millbrook Sound Studios, New York by Buck Dharma, Eric Bloom
Release date: June 2005
Running time: 50:54

While *Heaven Forbid* did not storm the charts, it generated sufficient interest to allow the band to make another album for CMC. It was another surprise that the new album followed so closely on the heels of the previous one.

Curse of the Hidden Mirror, whose name is borrowed from an old Stalk-Forrest Group song, follows much of the same recipe as *Heaven Forbid* in terms of production philosophy, and features nearly the same line-up. The only difference is that Chuck Bürgi is replaced by veteran drummer Bobby Rondinelli, whose past credits include classic Rainbow albums like *Difficult to Cure* and *Straight Between the Eyes*. He was also the uncredited drummer on Scorpions' platinum-selling *Love at First Sting* (if you've heard 'Rock You Like a Hurricane', you've heard Bobby), and he played on Black Sabbath's *Cross Purposes*. A hard-hitting drummer, Bobby is one of those musicians with hard rock in his blood.

Curse was a conscious attempt to move the clock back a little, something signalled both by the title of the album, which is evocative of the Pearlman days, and by the cover artwork by digital artist Ioannis, depicting an Egyptian scene involving the mysterious mirror. Whether that mirror is a conscious reference to Sandy's obsidian mirror from *Imaginos*, is uncertain. What is certain, is that the music also hails back to the band's glory days. Gone are the flirtations with thrash metal – this is old school hard rock, with plenty of Hammond playing from Allen this time around as well.

In an interview with *Popentertainment.com*, Donald shed some light on the thinking behind the album:

> *It's basically going with your strengths. For us to reinvent ourselves, it's not really necessary or desirable. Certainly, I think our best work is when we stay true to what our soul is, musically and stylistic wise. I like to think of it as closing your eyes and creating or closing your eyes and*

playing, that's what came out when we did that metaphorically. It was joyful. Rather than worrying about 'what am I gonna do in 2001, how's it going to fit in with the popular culture of the day?' I'm just not worrying about that at all at this point.

'Dance on Stilts' (Roeser, John Shirley)

It's Donald who throws the first punch on *Curse*, with the hard rock/pop amalgamation of 'Dance on Stilts'. The first thing that hits the listener is a very in-your-face sound, with a dry, chunky guitar sound and earth-shattering bass guitar. The drums are punchy, but perhaps overly compressed this time around.

I'm honestly not sure what the lyrics are about, but I'm going with an educated guess that dancing on stilts is a risky business and something one does to appear taller and tougher than one is.

The music is pretty standard fare, hard rocking riffs and catchy refrains, but it's not a standout Donald track unfortunately, and it is also over-long, clocking in at over 6 minutes. It's mostly saved by the energetic rhythm section and as such works better as an opener than it should, on purely musical merits.

'Showtime' (Bloom, John Trivers)

It might have been wiser to go with the next track as opener, as Eric's 'Showtime' really does sound like fairly classic BÖC. A co-write with his buddy John Trivers, 'Showtime' was originally written for *Cultösaurus Erectus*.

Confusingly, seeing as this is not a Shirley lyric, the narrative of the song is almost a step-by-step recounting of 'Power Underneath Despair' from the previous album, another story about a guy wrongfully imprisoned who waits for revenge.

It starts with some stinging blues licks before a sly groove is established by the whole band. As Eric's voice enters it becomes clear that it has lost some of the force that surprised us on *Heaven Forbid*. Still, a hard rock singer is allowed to grow gracefully older, and he has lost none of his expressiveness, even if the range and the lung force is not what it used to be. About two minutes and a half into the song it switches gears into a full-blown reggae for a brief moment. The song ends with an unusual guitar solo from Buck, economic and groove based, and with some backwards effects as the song fades out.

'The Old Gods Return' (Bloom, Roeser, Shirley)

Next up is one of the epic songs on the album, 'The Old Gods Return', clearly a reference to H. P. Lovecraft's universe. While the band's gutsy move to include quite a few proggy songs on the record is to be applauded, it is unfortunately in these ambitious numbers that the album falls short. While the musicianship is impeccable, the songwriting isn't quite strong enough to support these bigger ideas. In this song some production shortcomings also become apparent. *Curse* was the Cult's first all-digital recording, and when Donald's plucked electric guitar comes in after the intro, it sounds uncomfortably direct, as if it was plugged straight into the digital recorder and treated to digital effects in the aftermath – which was probably the case. It's a shame, because *Heaven Forbid* was such a nice-sounding record, with full, warm guitar sounds.

When Eric comes in, singing Shirley's sinister lyrics, there is also a conspicuous absence of proper melody, with Eric more talking than singing the wordy text. While the band grooves engagingly underneath, the song is sadly lacking in both melodic movement and interesting progressions. For all the progginess and strange effects, the song feels static. There are also too many repetitions, both of lyrics and riffs.

Towards the end of the song picks up, as Eric starts sounding more engaged and more like his old self, and Donald delivers his first truly engaging guitar solo on the album.

'Pocket' (Roeser, Shirley)

It's really only on the fourth track that the album gains proper momentum. 'Pocket' is classic Buck pop, smooth, catchy, clever and breezy. John Shirley's lyrics here are absolutely lovely, describing what in this day and age would be called 'mindfulness', but my generation would call it a 'zen moment', an experience of being 100% present in the moment and in your immediate environment:

> *The blossoms are falling,*
> *Making a white path across the grass*
> *Thunderheads are building, your skin tightens*
> *And you wait for the flash*
>
> *Across the street, the boys are laughing*
> *As they wash each other's cars*
> *They turn up the hip-hop*
> *White boys*
> *Rapping with the black stars*
>
> *Are you in the pocket of the moment in this particular second*
> *Screwed into the socket of the moment in this particular second*
> *Where time cannot be reckoned*
> *Are you in the pocket of the moment*

The song opens with a crisp guitar riff before it launches into the first verses. Donald sounds more effortless than ever, his singing mature and self-assured, and the melody floats across the upbeat guitars like wispy summer clouds. Just like with the best of Donald's songs, the music complements the lyrics perfectly. The production is also better here, the sound opening up, the guitars occasionally fanning out to give space to the Hammond organ. Donald's leads are excellent here, employing a bit of a surf sound and emphasising melody over shred. Around the three-minute mark the organ swells and the drums get frantic, building up to a small guitar crescendo before the last choruses call out, with gorgeous backing harmonies. A definite highlight on the album, 'Pocket' is a song that matches the best moments of *Heaven Forbid*, without maybe plunging quite the existential depths of 'Live For Me'.

'One Step Ahead of the Devil' (Bloom, Roeser, Danny Miranda, Bobby Rondinelli, Shirley)

The next song continues the positive trend. 'One Step Ahead of the Devil' is an exhilarating, hard-hitting song keeping a healthy pace and seeing Eric playing to his vocal strengths. Shirley's lyrics tell a tale of a man on the run, not just from the evil deeds of others, but also his own crimes.

> *You hear the darkness weeping*
> *For those who fall tonight*
> *That night you lay beside her, for once you almost slept*
> *Until her slim blade glimmered near got you 'fore you leapt*
> *Wish you could leave her livin but that's like guns and rust*
> *You don't want it on your gun, it's just like you and trust*

The sound here is quite reminiscent of the more straightforward moments of *Secret Treaties*, with a bit of a boogie swagger to the uncompromising riffage, and the Hammond pushing out between the guitar carnage. Bobby Rondinelli shines here, showing the true meaning of 'whipping the skins'. Even Donald steps back into his '70s mode, with his soloing tinged by Southern blues.

'I Just Like to be Bad' (Bloom, Bryan Neumeister, Shirley)

As if to outdo the previous song in '70s retrospection, 'I Just Like to be Bad' opens with some rock'n'roll piano from Allen that could have been straight out of *Agents of Fortune*. This song was co-written by Eric and Bryan Neumeister, who also had a hand in the song 'Eye of the Hurricane'. Not on the too-serious side, 'I Just Like to be Bad' is like a feminist re-reading of *Career of Evil*, with a female protagonist who takes what she wants, consequences be damned:

> *She said I just like to be bad*
> *First names only and one night stands*
> *I just like to be bad*
> *Forget the face, I want the hands*

While it doesn't offer any surprises or complexities, this is one of the better rockers on the album.

'Here Comes the Feeling' (Roeser, Dick Trismen)

We're back in breezy pop territory with 'Here Comes the Feeling', written by Donald and Dick Trismen, who also wrote the lyrics for 'Madness to the Method'. This is a song that borders on pure AOR and as such could have fit neatly with 'Dancin' in the Ruins' on *Club Ninja*. It's got that 'driving at night' propulsion that the best AOR hits seem to have, and it has enough variation and rhythmic interest to make up for the borderline cheesy lyrics. Donald's rhythm guitar work here is very nice, with echoes of Mick Jones' guitar playing on some of those Foreigner hits. There's also nice interplay going on between jaunty unison lines on bass and guitar and nicely syncopated drums. More than anything, the song shows what a sophisticated pop writer Donald had become at this point. Why he was never called upon to write songs for other pop singers is a bit of a mystery.

'Out of the Darkness' (Miranda, Bloom, Roeser, Shirley)

'Out of the Darkness' is the moodiest song on the album, with a slow pace, some atmospheric string synths and languid lead guitar. Shirley's lyrics are cryptic and suggestive without telling an outright story.

> *Out of the darkness out of the dust cloud*
> *Follow the thread and then trace your way free*
> *Your father, your mother have bound you in darkness*
> *Have blinded you sweetly and so far from me*
> *They cannot abide me, your father and mother*
> *But they cannot divide me from the one other than me*

The song is a decent dig at the cinematic, but one is left with the feeling that the BÖC of old would have injected the song with a lot more drama and dynamics. It feels a little pedestrian, and the vocal melody seems too bound to the underlying harmonic structure. On the upside we are treated to some truly delicious lead guitar work, again in that David Gilmour mode that Donald also employed on 'Cold Grey Light of Dawn'. After the guitar solo there is a very nice section with a staccato ostinato from the guitar and bass padded with Allen's synth. Danny Miranda makes the most out of the song with busy bass playing, while Rondinelli's funk-infused drumming is marred by a too prominent click on the bass drum – a problem throughout the album.

'Stone of Love' (Roeser, Meltzer)

For the next number, Donald dug deep in the archives to find 'Stone of Love', a song written in the early '80s and probably a contender for one of the Birch-produced albums back then. Richard Meltzer's lyrics for this song are highly poetic.

*There is a chain that I have worn
And on the chain a thorn is hung
There is a pain forever borne
That sings a song forever sung
The song is but a stone
Stone of love*

These are words that really bring the listener back to that intersection between the weird and romantic that made the band so special in the mid-'70s. The music is good too, with Donald in his more rhythmic mode, a slight funk to the riffs and a brisk tempo. That digital sound makes the guitars a tad too abrasive, and the song's simplicity does not warrant the almost six-minute running time – mostly due to extensive soloing. But the song shows a smoother, almost West Coast-side to the band's abilities, with Rondinelli occasionally switching to snappy rimshots instead of his rock-hard snare hits. The strummed acoustic fleshing out the arrangement is also a nice touch.

'Eye of the Hurricane' (Bloom, Neumeister, Roeser, Rondinelli, Shirley)

The most adventurous song on the album is the monumental 'Eye of the Hurricane'. This is the most successful of the 'epics' on the album, and also the song most reminiscent of what they were doing on the previous album. It starts characteristically with synthesized pizzicato strings and strains of guitar before it settles into a chugging guitar groove that is the closest we get to the thrash references on *Heaven Forbid*. Eric is totally in his element her, expressive, theatrical and menacing, and this song has all the drama that was lacking from 'Out of the Darkness'. There are thunderous drum fills and Wagnerian organ swells – in fact this is the one song on the album where Allen's presence is finally felt and really appreciated. The lyrics, again by Shirley, are intriguing too - presumably about trying to keep one's cool in the torrent of life:

*People fly around me like dead leaves in high wind
They stream down the choking streets and never quite reach the end
Sometimes I wear a blue buzzsaw, I wear it like mohawk steel
Sometimes I ride my fatal flaw blindfolded, do it by feel*

*He never blinks, he never blinks, he doesn't care what you think
Cause there's an eye in my hurricane*

Midways through the song a lone guitar over the synthesiser strings signals the arrival of the album's most infectious moment, a proggy breakdown with wild guitars, time changes, oozing Hammond and nice interplay. A true high point. 'Eye of the Hurricane' shows all the potential that was still in the band, and I can't help that thinking if the boys had spent a little more time pruning the material on the album, it could all have been of this high standard.

'Good to Feel Hungry' (Miranda, Bloom, Roeser, Shirley)
The album ends on a very strong note with the unusual 'Good to Feel Hungry', a song whose core idea came from Danny Miranda. Driven by an incredibly powerful and catchy bass-line and operating with some tricky time signatures (the verses are in an esoteric 10/8), the song is also augmented by nice, jazzy chord voicings from Donald. The song recalls the eclectic genre play of the debut album and *Agents of Fortune*. Allen even brings out a Doors-like organ sound for a great solo midways through the song. After the solo section the song is brought down to a bluesy hush with haunting vocals from Eric, before it explodes again with fiery guitars and pounding drums. In many ways the song encapsulates a lot of what has made the band great through the decades – the musical intelligence, the eclecticness and the playful groove. As such it is not just a worthy ending to the album, but – at least so far – an honourable endpoint for Blue Öyster Cult's recording career.

While *Curse of the Hidden Mirror* is a slight step backwards from the surprising energy of *Heaven Forbid*, it is still a worthy record and a remarkable achievement for a band so far into the twilight years of their career. Yes, Eric's voice is showing signs of age and the production is marred by what one could call 'digital optimism', the belief that new-fangled digital tools can replace time-honoured analogue devices. But it is also a brave record, and one that successfully merges the band's rich history with the energy and bravado of the then-current touring line-up.

While *Curse* made no indents in either charts or radio waves, it, like its predecessor, found favour with critics. The website Blistering wrote:

'So, for all of the storied history of the band BÖC has proven that they are anything but an oldies act coasting on past glories, in fact if these last two records prove anything it is that BÖC have many chapters left to write in their spell book.'

Internet music bible Allmusic positively glowed in their review, stating that '*Curse of the Hidden Mirror* is a remarkably consistent, subtle, and even poetic album that expands their sci-fi undercurrents without getting lost in space. It's far better than some of the group's limp late-'80s work and stands as one of the finest albums of their nearly three decade -- and counting -- career of evil.'

Not bad for a group of Long Island misfits who once got hi-jacked by the mystical prophet of the rock'n'roll revolution.

Appendix: The live recordings

This book is primarily dedicated to the official studio-recorded output of the band. Which is not to say that Blue Öyster Cult's live albums are not significant – but with a band that has played thousands and thousands of gigs throughout their career, the occasional scattering of live releases is hardly representative of what the band has sounded like at various times on stage. Nevertheless, in this appendix I will briefly mention some of the more significant live recordings.

The earliest, semi-official live recording from the band is also one of their best. The so-called *Bootleg EP* was a 1972 stereo recording from a bar in Rochester, New York, that Columbia decided to release as a promotional EP aimed at radio DJs just ahead of *Tyranny* & Mutation's release. It has since resurfaced in a number of guises, official and unofficial, and parts of it now appear both on the *Tyranny & Mutation* reissue as well as on various compilations. It shows the band in its formative phase, absolutely raw and unadorned, playing with immense power and conviction. On 'Cities on Flame' Albert's voice breaks constantly, but the song drips with menace and occult force, while 'Workshop of the Telescopes' is about as creepy as anything you'll ever hear. *The Bootleg EP* shows the side of the band that endeared them to the East Coast intelligentsia, the dirty, garage/proto-punk attitude coupled with clever, tongue-in-cheek writing. In many ways this live recording was never bettered.

The first live recording available to the record-buying public at large was the sprawling double album *On Your Feet or On Your Knees*, released in 1975 to cash in on the relative success of *Secret Treaties*. Double live-albums were de rigeur for '70s rock groups, and in retrospect it rarely seems like a good idea. Those albums were either padded with over-long drum solos, pointless covers or three-minute hits turned into 10-minute jams. *On Your Feet* doesn't entirely escape this megalomania, but it is on the whole a decent live document. The inclusion of two very long covers ('Born to Be Wild' and 'I Ain't Got You') is indeed superfluous, and large parts of the album suffer from muddled sound, but when it's good it's great. The version of 'Then Came the Last Days of May', with guitar that would make Mark Knopfler cry and booming analogue synth from Allen, is one highlight. 'ME 262' is also a killer, rough and visceral and lightning fast. And who could forget the rendition of '7 Screaming Diz-Busters', with its psychedelic jamming and Eric's satanic monologues ('I'm not talking about the light above, I'm talking about the hellfire down below…')?

All in all, *On Your Feet* was a worthy document of a band on the brink of serious success.

Next up, from 1978 and their super-stardom era, is perhaps their most widely lauded live release, *Some Enchanted Evening*. The sound is much improved, but I don't share the majority view of this album. For a single LP, and with such an abundance of great material to choose from, two cover songs are two too many – in this case MC5's 'Kick Out the Jams' and The Animals' 'We Gotta Get

Out of This Place'. What remains is then a solid but highly predictable selection of BÖC classics. The two softer numbers, 'Astronomy' and 'The Reaper', both fall short of their more richly textured studio siblings, but Donald's guitar blow-out at the end of 'Astronomy' is a thing of pure beauty. The best track on the album is probably 'E.T.I.', but even here it's no match for the studio version, sounding a little muffled with the drums pushed to the background. *Some Enchanted Evening*, with its beautiful cover artwork, was a commercial success, and I am sure fans appreciated hearing the 'hits' in live renditions. But I don't personally find that the album lives up to its reputation. The Columbia/Legacy reissue from 2007 is worthy of tracking down, as it contains a bonus CD and a live DVD from one of the concerts.

For an alternative view of this era of the band in concert, I would also recommend tracking down the old VHS concert simply titled *Blue Öyster Cult Live 1976*, which was released in 1991 by now defunct Castle Communications – also on CD. It was recorded on the *Agents* tour in Maryland. The sound is dubious, but the performances are great, and you get a better selection of *Secret Treaties* material.

1982's *Extraterrestrial Live*, a 2LP set, offered a much more comprehensive track selection, and a punchier sound. It is controversial among fans because it mostly features newcomer Rick Downey on drums, having primarily been recorded on the *Fire of Unknown Origin* tour after Albert's departure. And indeed, the two tracks Albert does appear on, 'Dominance and Submission' and 'Black Blade', are the best tracks of the lot. Opening track 'Dominance and Submission' captures all the live magic and energy of their shows, with Eric interacting with the audience and creating that dark, carnivalesque atmosphere that the fans loved during the concerts. It's remarkable how much more confident Eric sounds as a live performer on this live offering compared to the previous ones.

'Black Blade' offers an insight into the band's virtuoso and proggy side, with the band tackling the changes and dynamic shifts like seasoned pros, and Eric offering a once-in-a-lifetime vocal performance. There are other highlights, too. 'Veteran of the Psychic Wars' is darkly atmospheric, and the extended guitar solo section is probably one of Donald's greatest performances captured on tape. Talk about underrated guitar hero. Robby Krieger pops in for a guest appearance on the extended jam of 'Roadhouse Blues', while Allen puts in a memorable piano performance on 'Joan Crawford'. Of the official live releases, I would say *Extraterrestrial Live* offers the most comprehensive and best-sounding live version of the band.

It wouldn't be until 2002, in the interim between *Heaven Forbid* and *Curse of the Hidden Mirror*, that the band released a new official live document. *A Long Day's Night* was released on DVD and CD by CMC. The upside to this release is that it has a fantastic selection of songs, featuring deep cuts like 'Mistress of the Salmon Salt', 'Lips in the Hills' and 'Perfect Water'. The downside is that it caught the band in a bad period, sounding under-rehearsed and tired, very different from the usually energetic band that fans hear in concerts even today. I would not recommend this release except for completists.

My personal favourite live recording is one that started life as a bootleg circulating among fans, but which today can be sampled on the amazing box set that Columbia put out in 2012, entitled *The Columbia Albums Collection*. In any event that box set is a must for any fan of the band, featuring as it does all the classic albums nicely remastered, with a wealth of bonus material, a nice booklet and tons of hitherto unheard live material.

But to get back on track, several of the live tracks there are taken from the 1986 King Biscuit Flower Hour radio broadcast from Santa Monica, California. The line-up featured a very fresh Jon Rogers on one of his first live outings with the band, as well as drummer Jimmy Wilcox and keysman Tommy Zvoncheck, in addition to Eric and Donald. This is a killer show in all respects. The selection of material is great, with the *Club Ninja* tunes ('Shadow Warrior', 'White Flags' and 'Dancin' in the Ruins') given all the grit and liveliness they lacked on the album, and with lots of classics to boot. The new musicians really breathe new life into the band. Wilcox' drumming is amazing, so much better than Rick Downey's live performances, and Jon Rogers brings a vital element to the mix in addition to his bass playing: Very sturdy and pitch perfect backing vocals. Last but not least, I am very fond of what Tommy Zvoncheck brought to the band in a live setting. He adds a touch of majesty, of cosmic dimensions, if you will, with his huge-sounding synths. Check out 'Shadow Warrior', for instance, and see what he brings to the table. And in a classic like 'Godzilla' he adds energy with a fusion-like synth solo. Another highlight is his intro to 'Take Mc Away', which makes you think you've mistakenly put on an album by prog rock super group U.K. For fans who are not Bouchard Brothers purists, this Santa Monica recording offers one of the tightest performances from the band.

Bibliography

Brett Clement: *Modal Tonicization in Rock: The Special Case of the Lydian Scale* (Gamut 6/1, 2013, Newfound Press)

Morning Final (Blue Öyster Cult fanzine, ed. Bolle Gregmar), issues 1-14

Modern Recording, issue 9, Sept, 1977 (Cowan Publishing Corp)

Rock Candy, issue 8, June/July 2018 (Rock Candy Magazine Ltd)

Isaac Newton Phelps: *The iconography of Manhattan Island, 1498-1909* (Columbia University, 1928)

Michael E. Bell: *Vampires and Death in New England, 1784 to 1892* (Anthropology and Humanism vol. 31, issue 2, 2006)

Martin Popoff: *Agent of Fortune.* The Blue Öyster Cult Story (Wymer, 2016)